SL

720
.92
COH

Le Corbusier

LIBRARIES DIRECT 9.99
FE 200306
A32831

Jean-Louis Cohen

LE CORBUSIER

1887–1965

The Lyricism of Architecture in the Machine Age

TASCHEN

KÖLN LONDON LOS ANGELES MADRID PARIS TOKYO

Illustration page 2 ▶ Le Corbusier at his work in
the studio on rue Nungesser-et-Coli, Paris, ca.
1960
Illustration page 4 ▶ *The Dog and the Woman*,
drawing, 1951.

© 2004 TASCHEN GmbH
Hohenzollernring 53, D–50672 Köln
www.taschen.com

Edited by ▶ Peter Gössel, Bremen
Project managed by ▶ Swantje Schmidt, Bremen
Conception and layout by ▶ Gössel und Partner,
Bremen
Text edited by ▶ Christine Fellhauer, Cologne

© FLC/VG Bild-Kunst, Bonn 2004, of works by
Le Corbusier
© VG Bild-Kunst, Bonn 2004, of works by
Willi Baumeister

Printed in Germany
ISBN 3-8228-3535-8

To stay informed about upcoming TASCHEN
titles, please request our magazine at
www.taschen.com or write to TASCHEN America,
6671 Sunset Boulevard, Suite 1508, USA–Los
Angeles, CA 90028, Fax: +1-323-463.4442. We will
be happy to send you a free copy of our magazine
which is filled with information about all of our
books.

Contents

Introduction

Charles-Edouard Jeanneret, ca. 1911

Few architects have embodied the hopes and disillusionments of the industrial age as Le Corbusier did, nor have any quite so scandalized and outraged their contemporaries, with the possible exception of Adolf Loos for a certain period and Frank Lloyd Wright throughout his lifetime. For much of Le Corbusier's life, sarcasm and slander were the bedfellows of one of the rare architects whose widespread fame has made his a household name. Between the Fallet House, built in 1906–07, and his posthumous projects, the unremitting production spanning six decades never ceases to amaze. Le Corbusier built 75 edifices in 12 countries, and took on 42 major city-planning projects. He left behind 8,000 drawings, more than 400 paintings and pictures, 44 sculptures and 27 tapestry cartoons. He wrote 34 books, totaling some 7,000 pages, and hundreds of articles; he gave lectures and has left behind some 6,500 private letters, in addition to his voluminous business correspondence.

Le Corbusier came of age at the time when cars and airplanes were becoming a common means of transportation, thus he was one of the first professional architects to ply his trade on several continents at once, looming as an internationally recognized architect well ahead of the pack. But thanks to photogravure and the modern press, he also became a public figure whose sundry declarations often caused a stir. This all-round man, always eager to cultivate his public persona, encompassed all the tensions of the 20th century, but at the same time he bequeathed a body of work unique in its complexity. He was also a man of great personal loyalty. The friendships that he formed in his hometown would accompany him throughout his entire life. His mother, Marie-Amélie Jeanneret-Perret, and his musician brother, Albert, remained lifelong confidants, as well as correspondents, along with the writer William Ritter. His close ties to his earliest friends, Léon Perrin and Auguste Klipstein, were long-lasting, as were the friendships he would strike up later with such artists as Fernand Léger and Louis Soutter.

Europe as a Classroom

La Chaux-de-Fonds, the town in the Swiss Jura where Charles-Edouard Jeanneret was born in 1887—he did not adopt the pseudonym Le Corbusier until 1920—was so focused on the manufacture of watches that Karl Marx once referred to it as "one big watchmaking factory." The interaction between industry and the visual arts here would also form the basis of Jeanneret's professional activities. In this environment people believed in the educative virtues of geometrized form, an essential component of the Froebel teaching method that Jeanneret had been exposed to as a boy, just like the young Frank Lloyd Wright 20 years earlier. At the town's Art School, run by the painter Charles L'Eplattenier, permeated by the ideas of John Ruskin and the Arts-and-Crafts Movement, the young man was gradually weaned away from courses aimed at turning him into a carver, chaser and engraver of watchcases, towards architecture.

Yet the countless travels he embarked on throughout his life in Europe and beyond provided his most formative education. The highly personal map he drew of Europe

Opposite page:
Assembly, Chandigarh, India, 1951–62
View of the portico with enameled steel pivoting door measuring 7.7 x 7 meters.

features three kinds of place he visited between 1907 and 1912: cultural, industrial and folkloric centers. His first trip took him to Tuscany, where he produced subtle watercolors of the buildings of Pisa, Siena and Florence. He sought to penetrate the mysteries of the "language of stones," and developed an interest in decor, as well as in unusual buildings, like the Charterhouse of Galluzzo in Val d'Ema. He then went to Vienna and Paris, where the poster artist Eugène Grasset told him about the experiments of the Perret brothers, who were "putting concrete into wooden boxes with iron rods." No sooner had Auguste Perret set eyes on Jeanneret's sketches than he employed him for the next 15 months in his office, on the ground floor of the iconoclastic buildings located at no. 25a, rue Franklin. He took part in the design of Oran Cathedral, and in 1908 drew up plans for La Saulot hunting lodge in Sologne, central France. Perret helped to develop the young man's tastes, and introduced him to Gustave Eiffel's Garabit viaduct in the Massif central, as well as to the buildings of Anatole de Baudot and Henri Sauvage in Paris and those of Tony Garnier in Lyons.

In Paris, where he lived in an attic room on the Quai Saint-Michel, Jeanneret read Friedrich Nietzsche's *Thus Spoke Zarathustra* in 1908, as well as Ernest Renan's *Life of Jesus* and Edouard Schuré's *The Great Initiates*, a celebration of the prophets, a present from L'Eplattenier. The Nietzschean imperative "Become who you are!" would become his motto. Then L'Eplattenier sent him to Germany to study the innovations being made in the decorative and industrial arts, and to write a book titled *La Construction des villes*, with the aim of criticizing local conceptions and designs. Like Walter Gropius and Mies van der Rohe, he worked with Berlin architect Peter Behrens, then joined his brother, Albert, with Swiss choreographer Jacques Dalcroze, in the Garden City of Hellerau near Dresden, where he discovered the rigorous Neoclassicism of Heinrich Tessenow, architect of numerous buildings and the Festival Theater in that reformist community. In Munich he got to know the writer William Ritter, who helped him come to terms with the differences between Germanic and Latin culture.

Ritter, who was well acquainted with the Slavic world, advised him to go further east, which he did. His trip took him first to Prague, then to Serbia and Bulgaria, where he drew rural buildings. This journey had two high points, one in Constantinople, the other in Athens. The urban skyline of the Ottoman capital fascinated him, and he made countless drawings of it and of houses on steep hillsides. On the Acropolis, Jeanneret delighted in an architectural ensemble that would leave an indelible mark on him. After Greece, he discovered Pompeii, then Rome and the charming countryside around Hadrian's Villa in Tivoli.

On his return, Jeanneret recorded his impressions of his travels in an article in the newspaper *Feuille d'avis de la Chaux-de-Fonds*. His knowledge of cityscapes, monumental complexes and popular buildings, acquired on the spot, would fuel his subsequent projects, and Jeanneret drew up a thesaurus of urban, architectural and formal features that he made use of without any fetishism. His knowledge of architectural history in no way diminished his appreciation of the edifices of Antiquity and the Renaissance. Later, he would refer to the "lesson of Rome" and rail against the "venerable carcasses" of the Academy, which distorted it and rendered it sterile.

In Search of a "New Spirit" in Paris

As a reaction to the destruction of parts of France that were being invaded, in 1914, together with engineer Max du Bois, he conceived the "Dom-ino" house (the name

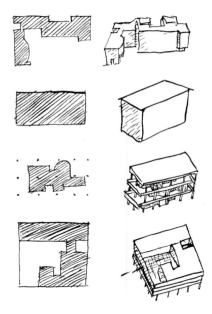

"Four compositions"
Illustration in *Le Corbusier et Pierre Jeanneret, Œuvre complète 1910 – 1929*, 1930.
From top to bottom: from the "somewhat facile genre" to the "very difficult," then to the "very facile" and lastly to the "very generous." These four are part of Le Corbusier's research undertaken in the 1920s (cf. p. 44).

having evolved from the Latin words *domus* [house] and *innovatio* [innovation]). Usually assembled in rows, either L- or U-shaped, like dominos, this involved above all a structural principle combining concrete uprights and slabs, thus opening up the greatest range of possibilities for the design of facades and the configuration of floor plans. He maintained close ties with Perret by letter, and undertook to write (but never completed) *France-Allemagne*, a book laying claim to French preeminence in the modern architectural movement. He spent 1915 poring over drawings and plans in books on city planning and gardens with a view to completing his book *La Construction des villes*, which he would end up abandoning.

Jeanneret settled in Paris in 1917, determined to conquer the city. At first he led the double life of an architect and an intellectual. The only project he realized was a water tower, set in a Bordeaux vineyard in Podensac with Neoclassical details. His frustration with his work caused him to call into question the postwar social movements and he tended to sympathize with reform-minded employers. Through Perret he met the painter Amédée Ozenfant, since 1915 editor of the review *L'Elan*, who gave him confidence in his abilities as a painter. They exhibited their works together in 1918 at the Thomas Gallery in Paris. To accompany the show, Ozenfant and Jeanneret published *Après le cubisme*, a manifesto in which they posited a somewhat ambiguous aesthetic program. In it they praised "objects of the most perfect banality [which have] the advantage of a perfect readability and of being recognized without effort, they avoid dispersion, the deviation of attention." While Jean Cocteau was that same year extolling French and Latin virtues in *Cock and Harlequin*, the two associates were comparing Greek architecture with modern factories.

In 1920, together with the poet and Dadaist promoter Paul Dermé, Jeanneret and Ozenfant published *L'Esprit nouveau*, an "illustrated international review of contemporary activity," and a forum for their theories and criticism. Its title was borrowed from a poem by Guillaume Apollinaire. The 28 issues of the review, the last of which appeared in 1925, enabled Ozenfant and Jeanneret, the latter adopting the pseudonym

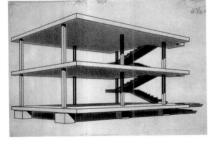

"Dom-ino" house, 1914
Perspectival view

Amédée Ozenfant, Albert Jeanneret and Le Corbusier in the studio at the Villa Jeanneret-Perret, 1919

Le Corbusier in the first issue (echoing his forbear Lecorbésier and possibly the painter Le Fauconnier), to report on current political, artistic and scientific developments. The visual world of *L'Esprit nouveau* was akin to that of the canvases painted by Jeanneret from 1919 onward. Thanks to Ozenfant, he met such artists as Juan Gris, Fernand Léger and Jacques Lipchitz, and attended the important art sales of Kahnweiler and Uhde, where he bought Cubist works on behalf of the Basel-based banker Raoul La Roche. As part of the "return to order" undertaken during the war, Ozenfant and Jeanneret sought a purified, refined language, like that of the Cubists, but rejected the distinction between art and everyday objects as well as any decorative tendencies. To highlight formal constants, they constructed their pictures from assemblages of *objets-types*: the curvaceous volumes of carafes, bistro glasses, piles of plates, guitars and pipes entered into a dialogue with rectangular books and dice. These family portraits of the mechanical age, also known as *agencements organiques*, embodied order and economy, but they also conjured up a classical tranquillity through their color range drawn from Greek Antiquity.

The review enjoyed an international readership, and in it Le Corbusier published a number of articles that would later be compiled in anthologies, such as *Vers une architecture* of 1923. In 1925 he published *Urbanisme*, *L'Art décoratif d'aujourd'hui* and, coauthored with Ozenfant, *La Peinture moderne*. The final issue of *L'Esprit nouveau*, no. 29, was turned into an *Almanac of Modern Architecture* in 1926. *Vers une architecture* was swiftly translated into German and English and, through bold comparisons, introduced links between the mechanical and art worlds, opening up new lines of thought for a readership that comprised more than just architects. In associating the Parthenon with the Delage automobile, Le Corbusier suggested that there is a comparable beauty in stone that has been hewn by a sculptor and a "mechanical organ." His "reminders" to "Messrs. Architects" about the virtues of the ground plan, surface and volume went hand in hand with an effort to open "eyes that don't see" to machines, such as airplanes, cars and ships. On the other hand he never forgot to look back in history or to emphasize the "lesson of Rome" and the importance of "regulating layouts," on which the proportions of Notre Dame in Paris and the Porte Saint-Denis had been based, whose continued relevance he acknowledged.

At the Bedside of Sick Cities

In the 1920s, his architectural production developed in two completely different directions. On the one hand, he continued his series of "Dom-ino" studies begun in 1914. On the other hand Le Corbusier designed—alongside his building projects marked by an economy of means—projects connected with specific sites for unconventional, well-off clients, who often came to him by way of *L'Esprit nouveau* and exhibitions. As a man and an architect with a proclivity to provoke, Le Corbusier swiftly became an iconoclastic city planner. The slogans of *Vers une architecture* were followed by those of *Urbanisme*, which denounced the "corridor street." Challenging the "medical" approach, whereby European city planners reckoned they would cure the "ills" of big cities, he advocated a radical "surgery," breaking with his own notions of the picturesque. Alongside this grand design, Le Corbusier would nevertheless take every opportunity to formulate more modest projects on sites with a more realistic topography.

Armed with his first manifestoes, he held countless lectures in Europe. Many of his trips ended by working on a plan. In 1930, the Soviet authorities consulted him on the

"Il faut tuer la rue-corridor!"—"Kill the corridor street!"
from *Précisions sur un état présent de l'architecture et de l'urbanisme*, 1930. Reproduction of a plate from the lectures delivered by Le Corbusier in South America in 1929.

decentralization of recreational facilities. His "response to Moscow," later named "La Ville radieuse," made room for industrial production, which was a novelty in his plans. The city's administrative center was now clearly separated from the residential neighborhoods, which he envisaged as a "green city." The lecture tour he made in South America in the autumn of 1929 totally transformed his perception of cities and landscapes. He no longer discovered them at ground level, like Florence and Rome, but from an airplane. His fascination with aeronautics, shown by his illustrated book *Aircraft*, published in English in London in 1935, led him frequently to use this kind of transportation. Struck by the sight of pampas and the great rivers of South America, he sketched master plans for Buenos Aires, Montevideo and São Paulo, followed by Algiers.

These activities were inextricably linked to his involvement in employer and technocratic circles, which turned his admiration for everything technical into a keen interest in the kind of leadership and rationalization of society then propagated by the technical elite. He was forever trying to persuade the "Authorities" to take radical steps to enable the "mobilization" of land, that is, to expropriate it in order to carry out his grand plans. After having identified between 1928 and 1931 with the Five-Year Plan of the Soviet Union, he included the Plan Obus for Algiers in his ambiguous modernization strategy supported by the reviews *Plans* and *Prélude*, to which he contributed between 1931 and 1936. The alternative between "Americanization" and "Bolshevization" then seemed to him to typify the situation in Europe. The idea of the "linear industrial city" borrowed from the Russians and used for the urban plan for the Zlín Valley in Moravia, in 1935 would become one of the "three human establishments," the latest theoretical system devised by Le Corbusier, which was published in 1945.

After juggling between large, unrealizable projects, which may have been destructive but galvanizing, and small-scale projects on real sites, after 1945 he worked on only a few, albeit concrete commissions. In the meantime, the occupation of France by the Germans saw him busily trying to persuade the various departments of the Vichy government of the wisdom of his ideas. He was successful in his publishing ventures, such as the publication in 1943 of *La Charte d'Athènes*, a handbook of functional city planning, before contributing to the thinking of Resistance fighters to forge a new country after the liberation.

Surprises during the Mature Years

With his 60th birthday behind him, and basking in world fame, Le Corbusier embarked on a new life. Like the construction of the United Nations Headquarters in New York City, based on his ideas, but executed by others—he reckoned he had been "stripped of all his rights as if in a forest"—the reconstruction of Europe was unsuccessful in his eyes because he failed to have any of his city-planning projects executed there. He did, however, manage to build in Marseilles the first Unité d'habitation, or housing complex, a prototype of the large apartment building that he had been toying with since 1922. He started making sculptures, with the help of cabinetmaker Joseph Savina in 1946, and then tapestry cartoons in 1948; he also developed his theory of the "synthesis of the major arts." By breaking with the celebration of technical aesthetics, he strove to create an "inexpressible space," an architectural synthesis that went beyond the analysis of engineers. He went to great lengths to lend more coherence to his works by formulating the "Modulor," a system of universal proportions based on the golden section and the human scale, which would underpin all his projects up until

Cover of *Aircraft*, published in London in 1935

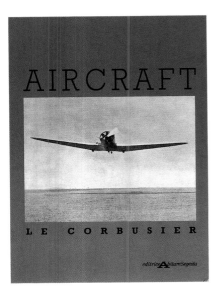

Le Corbusier, ca. 1960

1965. In tandem the books that he published, such as *Les Plans de Paris, L'Atelier de la recherche patiente* and *Le Poème de l'angle droit*, were no longer manifestoes but aesthetically appealing objects, incorporating all the aspects of his lines of thinking, in which theoretical involvement often gave way to autobiography.

When he conceived the sculptural Ronchamp church in 1951–55, and then again when he used vernacular building systems for the Jaoul Houses in those same years, he shocked those who had pigeonholed him in the white aesthetics and Platonic volumes of the 1920s. Thanks to the trust invested in him by Indian prime minister Jawarhalal Nehru, he finally managed to design an entire city from scratch, Chandigarh, and realize administrative buildings of the Punjab. At the same time he erected two houses and a building in Ahmedabad in which he made clever use of the climate and light of India with his favorite themes. With projects as far-flung as Japan, where he built the National Museum of Western Art in Tokyo in 1959, and the United States, where he designed the Carpenter Center for the Visual Arts for Harvard University in 1959–62, Le Corbusier also had a habit of spending his summers rather like a hermit, in the small wooden house he built beside the Mediterranean in Roquebrune-Cap Martin or in his studio on rue Nungesser-et-Coli in Paris.

His final projects show no signs of self-indulgence or complacency, but instead are marked by a fertile restlessness of his early years. They engaged in a dialogue with spirituality, as in the Dominican Monastery of La Tourette and the unfinished Church of

Firminy. They explored new kinds of technical and aesthetic possibilities, as in the Philips Pavilion at the 1958 Exposition universelle in Brussels. But they were also the result of a process of reminiscence, in which Le Corbusier updated the themes of his initial work, such as the "architectural promenade" and the "open plan," and rediscovered cities that had once won his heart, like Venice, with his hospital project. Up until his death, in 1965, his work remained reflective and was inspired by his memories of landscapes and buildings he had once seen, as well as by his own creative works.

Duality and Multiplicity

Throughout his long career, Le Corbusier was associated with the Unité d'habitation and the Ronchamp church, as well as with acerbic remarks, for which he was never at a loss, and which would take on a more and more melancholic tone as the years passed. But if one tries to understand his personality as it was in the 1920s, he was also a manufacturer, a painter—even if he reckoned he had been "rejected by professional painters"—a critic and essayist, a reporter and a decorator. The well-rounded personality that he presented to the public was forever being reinvented. In a letter written in 1926, he revealed an internal duality: "Le Corbusier is a pseudonym. Le Corbusier produces architecture, and that's all. He pursues unmotivated ideas. . . . He is an entity detached from the weight of flesh and blood. He must (but will he manage as much?) never wane. Ch. Edouard Jeanneret is the man of flesh and blood who has been through all the radiant and desperate adventures of a rather turbulent life. Jeanneret Ch. E. makes paintings, for, not being a painter, he has always been passionately interested in painting, and has always painted." It is this duality that makes his most radical edifices engaging, and broadens the outlook of his paintings.

The circle in which Le Corbusier developed encompassed several generations, starting with father figures like L'Eplattenier and Auguste Perret, who was incidentally only ten years his senior, Peter Behrens, whom Le Corbusier would turn his back on, and Munich architect Theodor Fischer, for whom he had undying respect and affection. His contact with Ludwig Mies van der Rohe was sporadic and with Walter Gropius somewhat more intense. Le Corbusier supported the Bauhaus program and became involved, together with Gropius, in the Congrès internationaux d'architecture moderne (CIAM) between 1928 and 1959 to promote radical ideas among the international elite. He was a close friend of the Zurich art historian and CIAM secretary general Sigfried Giedion, but his relations with some of the French CIAM members, such as André Lurçat, were more difficult. Certain faraway contacts were also important, such as those established with Aleksandr Vesnin and the Russian Constructivists in 1928, and, in Brazil, Lucio Costa and the young Rio architects Oscar Niemeyer and Affonso Eduardo Reidy. Le Corbusier's relationship with Frank Lloyd Wright, with whose work he had become acquainted at a very early stage, was always distant, for Wright seemed to be jealous of the Parisian's charisma, so much so that he fiercely criticized Le Corbusier's Marseilles Unité d'habitation.

In his circle of close friends, Pierre Jeanneret, Charlotte Perriand and Jean Prouvé stood out from the rest, for they were politically rather leftwing and distanced themselves from Le Corbusier in the late 1930s mainly for political reasons. The network of former studio draftsmen in rue de Sèvres thus formed a close-knit group spanning generations. Pierre-André Emery, Alfred Roth, Josep Lluís Sert and Junzo Sakakura were important studio figures prior to 1940. Gérald Hanning, André Wogenscky, Georges

The "Modulor," 1955
Watercolor hanging in Le Corbusier's "little studio" on rue de Sèvres: study for an illustration in *Le Poème de l'angle droit*

Le Corbusier Center, Zurich, Switzerland,
1963–67
Overall view

Candilis and Roger Aujame ensured the continuation of the office after 1945. Yannis Xenakis, Balkrishna Doshi and Jean-Louis Véret, followed by José Oubrerie, Guillermo Jullian de la Fuente and many more, helped to realize projects in the last ten years of his life, as well as posthumously, for the projects that had not been executed during the architect's lifetime.

From Scandal to Recognition

From the moment L'Esprit nouveau burst onto the world stage, Le Corbusier became a public figure, or rather a host of public figures. His iconoclastic articles made him first a Nietzschean rebel and then a nihilist destroyer, before his first constructions helped Russian leaders see in him "the epitome of the new man." He was mocked by Salvador Dalí, and to the anticommunist critics he was "the Trojan Horse of Bolshevism." In the eyes of the detractors of his Unité d'habitation in Marseilles he became the "madman" or the "brute" of béton brutal (rough concrete) after 1945. The art historian Pierre Francastel reproached him for wanting to force happiness on the occupants of his buildings by adopting an almost totalitarian approach.

In the 1950s, Le Corbusier was indisputably a celebrity, yet he was more or less overlooked by French officialdom until André Malraux, then Minister of Culture, commissioned him in extremis to build the museum he had been wanting to create for the past 30 years. In those years, when his style was used universally in what was at times a caricatural formalist way, the critical range and the rigor of his work from the Purist years were rediscovered by architectural critic Colin Rowe and several young American architects, such as John Hejduk, Peter Eisenman and Richard Meier. This marked the beginning of a whole new development—one that is still taking place— propelled by architectural historians striving to reconstruct from archival material a painstaking genealogy of his projects and ideas. From then on, nothing would elude scholars, from the most subtle episodes of Le Corbusier's boyhood to the most secret ins-and-outs of his relations with the "Authorities."

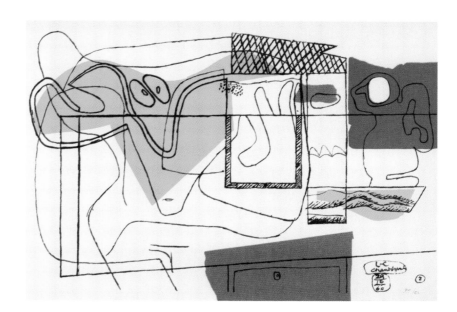

Alraça, a lithograph from the Cortège
collection, 1962

"The woes of living made human and the
disdain for the woes of living incarnated in
the soul of the great condor," Christmas card
Jeanneret sent to his parents, 1909
John Petit, *Le Corbusier lui-même*, 1970

Le Corbusier's posthumous fame took on such startling dimensions that some of his unrealized designs may yet be executed. The "L'Esprit nouveau" Pavilion was meticulously reconstructed in Bologna, and the church in Firminy was fairly accurately studied before his death, so that it could be erected; the Errazuriz House, designed in 1930 for Chile, and the Governor's Palace in Chandigarh would, on the other hand, be little more than life-size, soulless maquettes if they were actually built.

Is it possible to formulate the thrust of Le Corbusier's "message," who throughout his life was driven by a prophetic fervor? His legacy indisputably consists of many different legacies and does not include any such thing as a Corbusian "tool box," no set of procedures that would make it possible to realize his designs. His own "transmission"—from idea to building—involved completely different entities, ranging from building components to edifice types and spatial configurations. But it is in his solutions to problems of the most complex projects that his many years of experience become most readily apparent. Le Corbusier himself seemed, furthermore, to practice a certain Mannerism when he reused some of his designs by distorting them, the way Michelangelo did with his early Renaissance motifs.

Le Corbusier's career could probably be summed up as a series of divergent if not contradictory stances. It was based on an indefatigable curiosity with regard to the city and its transformations, to the history of architecture and to the vernacular. In a way his career was also logocentric, for his architecture is declared and revealed through the written word, which explains his intentions. It was because he was capable of theorizing that Le Corbusier was an acknowledged innovator. But his career also demanded political action. He may have entertained the illusion of being able to persuade the most varied of decisionmakers of the rightness and necessity of his theses, but this was above all because he was conscious of the responses that architecture could elicit in the face of urban problems. Nobody was less "Corbusian" than Le Corbusier himself. Far from confining himself to a single style, even if it were his, he challenged his own architectural discourse on many occasions.

1906–1907 ▸ Fallet House

Chemin de Pouillerel, La Chaux-de-Fonds, Switzerland
▸ with René Chapallaz

Detail of the gable wall

Plan of the ground floor

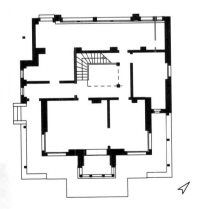

It did not take long before the manufacture of watches proved to be too limited a field for the young Jeanneret, whose mind soon focused on other activities. With architect René Chapallaz, who had helped his former teacher L'Eplattenier to design his residence on a hill overlooking his hometown, Jeanneret built a house for the master engraver Louis Fallet in 1906–07 on a nearby plot. The building permit, which was applied for by Chapallaz in 1906, described a compact building in the stereotypical chalet style that had shaped Swiss national identity for decades.

Set on sloping ground facing south, this solid block sheltered by a two-hipped ridge roof was, it would seem, first conceived as a maquette. The center of its symmetrical plan is occupied by a two-story entrance hall containing the staircase. The large living room opens on to the valley through an enclosed loggia supporting the bedroom balcony. The vertical distribution of the rooms did not introduce any innovations to Swiss middle-class homes of the day: the basement housed the utility rooms, the main floor the reception rooms and the upper floor the bedrooms.

The unusual aspect of the house lies in its interior decoration, which is treated as an integral part of the structure itself. L'Eplattenier had acquainted his pupils with John Ruskin's thinking on landscape, and had had them reproduce illustrations from Owen Jones' *Grammar of Ornament*. But above all he had urged them to discover the world around them. So Jeanneret drew Jura landscapes and local plant life, fir trees in particular, from which he derived the geometric figures carved on his watchcases, and animal forms, such as in the bee on a watchcase of 1906.

The natural motifs featured in many of his drawings are ubiquitous in the Fallet House. The stout brackets, made of Jura stone, supporting the main floor resemble crystal formations, conjuring up the forms carved on the 1906 watch. The wall surfaces and in particular the gables are decorated with sgraffito embellishments reproducing stylized motifs of fir trees and their cones, as well as trees in their winter state, on the lower half of the windows. Moreover, the ironwork is adorned with a triangular form reminiscent of conifers, a shape that recurs in the wall paneling. A warm, red-, yellow- and blue-based color scheme lends the whole edifice an almost oriental look.

This first work, which was acclaimed by the inhabitants of La Chaux-de-Fonds, earned Jeanneret and Chapallaz the commission for two villas on adjoining plots, one for Albert Stotzer, a watchcase polisher, and another for Ulysse-Jules Jacquemet, a teacher at the watchmaking school. Both these homes were designed in Vienna and completed in 1908. They drew on the principles of the first house, but took on a more solid and rigid form, using reinforced-concrete floors, thus representing a reproducible prototype. Meanwhile, the fees received for the Fallet House enabled Jeanneret to embark on his first extended trip through Europe.

Opposite page:
House viewed from the garden
The geometric design of the woodwork echoes the sgraffito on the gable wall.

1912 ▸ Villa Jeanneret-Perret
Chemin de Pouillerel, La Chaux-de-Fonds, Switzerland

The pergola, ca. 1918
In the foreground, Jeanneret's parents; in the background, the two brothers, Albert and Charles-Edouard

Plan of the ground floor

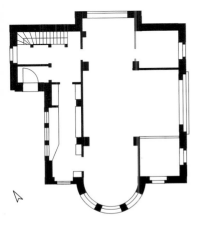

Opposite page:
House viewed from the garden

Back in La Chaux-de-Fonds, after discovering much of German-speaking Europe as well as the Balkans and the Mediterranean, Jeanneret divided his time between teaching at the "new department" of the town's Art School and working as an architect and decorator. He produced several innovative furniture collections for a group of Israeli clients, and worked on urban-development projects, most notably the Les Crêtets Garden City, which is clearly indebted to Heinrich Tessenow's Garden City in Hellerau.

On a plot of land near the houses built with Chapallaz, he introduced a new approach to design in the "white villa," which he built for his parents. Here the ground plan was not squeezed into a preconceived form, as was the case with the chalet. The house was not set on a promontory, but perpendicular to the slope, on a site bounded by a retaining wall. From the road the house can be reached by way of a long walk, first sheltered by a pergola—like those drawn by Jeanneret in Pompeii—then, after a right turn, covered by trees and ending at the well-concealed front door.

The door opens onto a small cloakroom, lit by a porthole window, and the stairwell. A hall then leads to the area containing the reception rooms, arranged on an axis running from the dining room, which opens onto the garden through an apse-like window, to the anteroom. This affords a view through the "large window overlooking the forest," by way of the living room on the slope side, lit by a rectangular, "large window with a view of the skyline." The corners house the small salon and the library. On the upper floor, the bedrooms are lit by a strip of windows whose horizontal extension call to mind Frank Lloyd Wright's Winslow House, in River Forest, Illinois, which Jeanneret had become acquainted with through German publications.

With its white plaster and roof made of asbestos-cement, but also its similarity—at least from certain angles—to the residences he had designed for sites on the Bosporus the year before, the Villa Jeanneret-Perret betrays the intensity of the architect's experiences in Italy and the East. The use of the land accords with the principles espoused by German architect Paul Schultze-Naumburg in his nine-volume work of 1906 entitled *Kulturarbeiten* (Cultural Works). Moreover, the details of the house reflect Paul Mebes' attempts to rehabilitate the simple, "honest" architectural forms current "around 1800."

Between the German Reformkultur and Mediterranean classicism, with which Jeanneret had become familiar by reading such publications as Charles Cingria-Vaneyre's *Entretiens de la Villa du Rouet* (Conversations at the Villa Le Rouet) of 1908, a personal approach to design began to take shape—albeit not without a certain awkwardness—that is quite exceptional for a young man who had just turned 25. The villa built at Le Locle that same year for Georges Favre-Jacot, owner of Zénith watches, confirms his rejection of earlier Jura models. Alongside features borrowed from Parisian mansions, echoes of contemporary German architecture come to the fore; the volume recalls the buildings of Schultze-Naumburg and Mebes, and the facade and arrangement of rooms the houses of Peter Behrens.

1916 ▸ Villa Schwob
Rue du Doubs, La Chaux-de-Fonds, Switzerland

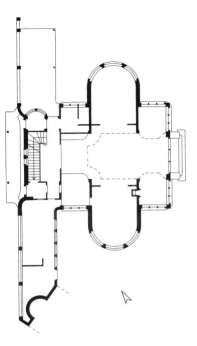

Plan of the ground floor

Opposite page:
View from the street

The living room with a view into the garden

The Villa Schwob, called the "Turkish villa" by neighbors, is the last building constructed by Jeanneret in La Chaux-de-Fonds. It is also the only one of his early houses that he deemed fit to write about in *L'Esprit nouveau*. With the Scala Cinema, completed that same year, he had erected his first building in the town center. This vast hangar of a structure made of concrete and timber on sloping ground has a roof that evokes Heinrich Tessenow's Festival Theater, which Jeanneret had seen in Hellerau, but the young architect also sought the advice of Auguste Perret for this work.

The large house built for the industrialist Anatole Schwob, owner of Cyma watches, is more radical than any of his earlier projects, and represents both a kind of recapitulation of his years of training and a harbinger of his shift to abstraction in the 1920s. Jeanneret departed from the concrete "bottle house" conceived in Perret's office in 1909, as he wrote to his mentor in 1916, telling him that it would have "French-style facades with terraces, but with reinforced concrete."

He duly used "the concrete framework erected in a few weeks and fillings made of pretty bare bricks," like the side facade of Perret's Théâtre des Champs-Elysées, whose main, square facade was borrowed for the large white surface of the building on rue du Doubs. The simple cubic volume with semicylindrical extensions represents the architect's final rejection of vernacular and classical forms found in his early works. The exterior retains a "touch of Istanbul," with the concrete elements replacing the timber components of the Ottoman constructions. But the interior incorporates references to several sources of inspiration, taking them a step further.

The sequence of rooms leading from the entrance to the two-story living room, betrays affinities with two sketches made by the architect in 1911 in Pompeii, and seems to reproduce the plan of the so-called Diomedes Villa, which is arranged around an atrium. It is difficult to distinguish this from other sources of inspiration for this design—which Le Corbusier would continue to stand by in his later years: the two-story English entrance hall, illustrated in British and German publications, the great empty space of a Parisian artist's studio, whose large window here affords a view of the garden, as well as the nave-like garage built by Auguste Perret on rue de Ponthieu in Paris in 1908, all documented in photographs of the construction site. The living room is the real center of the house. It accommodates the grand piano, and is situated at the intersection of the lengthwise axis leading from the entrance to the garden and the crosswise axis. This latter links the games room and the dining room on the ground floor. Upstairs, the two bedrooms form a U around the central void of the entrance hall. The kitchen is pushed to the outside, against the street wall, and the bathrooms upstairs are wedged between the bedrooms and the staircase.

Writing to Ritter in June 1920, Jeanneret saw in this house the springboard for a new program encompassing his travel memories. "I am busy with serious, indeed scholarly works, that is paintings that should at least represent extensions of my Villa Schwob.... But my attention is drawn to the Parthenon and to Michelangelo....A flawless art. And of a curbed temperament: another model—the Parthenon, that drama."

1923 ▸ Villa La Roche-Jeanneret

Square du Docteur-Blanche, Paris, France

Overall view of the Villa La Roche

The semi-detached house designed in 1923 for Raoul La Roche and Albert Jeanneret in the Paris suburb of Auteuil marked a turning point in Le Corbusier's architectural thinking, mindful as he was of the movements of the European avant-garde. The first designs for a site located in a middle-class neighborhood that then still had a village atmosphere were nothing more than property speculation—like so many of the small projects that Le Corbusier worked on in Paris. A more modest program eventually emerged, and the initial sketches of symmetrical ground plans were abandoned. This project actually marks the point at which Le Corbusier began to turn his attention to the work of his European contemporaries. Despite this fact, however, he was now hostile to much German architecture—although he did support the Weimar Bauhaus at the time of its closure—and he showed little sensitivity to the subtle differences

Opposite page:
The gallery in the Villa La Roche, seen from the entrance hall

Right:
The ramp in the gallery of Villa La Roche

The living room in the Villa Jeanneret
On the wall, a painting by André Bauchant

Plan of the ground floor of the two villas

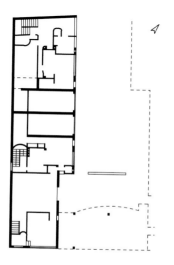

between the various Russian avant-garde movements, despite his correspondence with Ilya Ehrenburg and El Lissitzky.

Yet he was so enthusiastic about the maquettes of Theo van Doesburg and Cornelis van Eesteren, "architects of the De Stijl group," exhibited at the "L'Effort moderne" gallery in Paris in October 1923 that he duly revised the principles according to which he had hitherto designed dwellings. After studying their "counter-compositions," he modified the La Roche-Jeanneret project, replacing the small windows with much larger ones. The house turned into a collage of large, flat expanses, either solid or glazed, and the conventional windows now converged at the edges of the respective room or building. His houses now suggested a break with all that came before them, establishing a prototype for house and home.

In other respects, the sequence of indoor spaces of the La Roche-Jeanneret House, culminating in the ramp leading to the picture gallery, is arranged like an "architectural promenade." Here, Le Corbusier implemented for the first time an idea that had occurred to him while inspecting the Acropolis in Athens—a theater for processions—like that put forward by Auguste Choisy in his *Histoire de l'architecture* (History of Architecture) of 1899. A walk up the ramp offers views that open up in three directions: upwards, horizontally and downwards. When climbing the stairs from the entrance, the full breadth of the hall can be appreciated and its relationship to the dining room is revealed. Once on a level with the crown of trees, among which the house is carefully

The library-cum-living room of the Villa La Roche
Located above the entrance hall, this area is reached via the gallery ramp

Plan of the first floor of the two houses

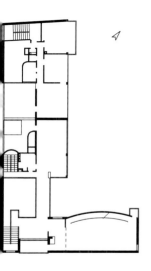

sited, the ramp leads to the picture gallery, whose curved wall supports a stairway leading to the roof terrace. It offers a well-lit setting for the Cubist and Purist canvases purchased by Le Corbusier and Ozenfant on behalf of La Roche.

The new formal working methods explored in this house saw Le Corbusier abandoning the constructive rationalism of Auguste Perret, still evident in the "Domino" house, and tackling the deployment of surfaces devoid of any structural function. The house's irregularity is justified by the fact that "each organ springs up alongside its neighbor, in accordance with an organic reason; the inside stretches out, determining the shape of the outside, which forms various saliences." This type of deductive composition, in which the plan is the "generator" that defines the house's volumes, echoes the approach of the late 19th-century French rationalists. But the irregularity is tempered by the presence of a formal principle that regulates the relations between the building's various components. While new spaces were conceived and assembled inside, the proportions of the volumes and outside apertures were defined by "regulating lines" using the golden section that also prescribes the dimensions and location of each element.

1923–1925 ▸ Villa "Le Lac"

Route de Lavaux, Corseaux (Vevey), Switzerland

The living room

Plan

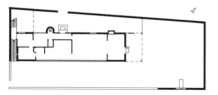

Once Le Corbusier was firmly established in Paris, his ties with Switzerland loosened, though he did spend time with his fellow countrymen living in Paris, like publisher Daniel Niestlé and banker Raoul La Roche. For his parents, who had been forced to sell their "white villa" in La Chaux-de-Fonds, he built a "little house" on the shores of Lake Geneva, in Corseaux, near Vevey. Although modest in size, this home represents a significant milestone in the architect's thinking about domestic spaces and landscapes.

This white-washed bungalow—in the shape of a simple parallelepiped—has a "single window 11 meters long" on the lakeward side. This "links and lights" and "brings into the house all the grandeur of a magnificent site." This "ribbon window" principle would be fiercely criticized by Auguste Perret, for whom "a window is a person," and hence, perforce, a vertical opening. This difference of opinion would rumble on until 1925.

When seen from the outside, the strip window calls into question the framing of the traditional *veduta*, "extending" the perspectival composition conceived in the

The house sited in the landscape, sketch

Renaissance that has shaped the perception of landscape ever since. It transforms the house's three main rooms—the two bedrooms and the living room—into a panoramic observatory overlooking the lake with a view of Mont Blanc, which towers above the far shore.

Inside, the rooms are lit by the ample daylight admitted through the windows, which turns domestic order on its head, for it illuminates dark nooks and crannies, eliminating the shadows normally cast in a house and implementing the "Ripolin Law," put forth by Le Corbusier in 1925 in *L'Art décoratif d'aujourd'hui* (*The Decorative Art of Today*, 1987) to justify the white walls. The dark areas and eclectic *objets-sentiments* (objects that elicit feelings) that one finds in traditional houses here give way to *objets-outils*, tools or practical objects that are fully lit.

On the "shore strip" where the house stands, Le Corbusier created on one side another unroofed space. Like a "walled enclosure," it contains "a green salon, an interior" painted white, for which—in a kind of antithesis to the solution used in the house and as if to underscore the bold design—a square window "limits the landscape, and dimensions it as the result of a radical decision."

Le Corbusier would return to the shores of Lake Geneva in 1926 with his project for the competition for the headquarters of the League of Nations in Geneva, which was rejected on the basis of technical quibbles. He used pilotis so as to "make the light shine beneath the buildings" of this huge complex of offices and conference rooms, and designed the long windows and terraces such that they "confront the entire site." This response to the Lake Geneva landscape went further, boasting "that pure horizontal at the top, sometimes detached from the sky, sometimes squaring up against the mountains soaring above them, that horizontal [that] was a lyrical kind of conclusion," as he wrote in 1928 in his avenging pamphlet *Une Maison, un palais* (A House, A Palace).

General view from the lake

1924–1926 ‣ Modern Frugès Quarter

Rue Le Corbusier, rue Henri-Frugès, rue des Arcades, Pessac, France

The "skyscrapers," 1925

In 1923, Le Corbusier concludes his book *Vers une architecture* (*Towards a New Architecture*, 1927) by posing the question "Architecture or revolution?" which he answers with "Revolution can be avoided." He thus asserted his commitment to the social virtues of low-cost housing. In spite of these magnanimous declarations, Le Corbusier would have only two opportunities to construct low-cost dwellings, both in the Bordeaux area. The first was a workers' community attached to a sawmill, built in 1923–24 in Lège-Cap-Ferret for the industrialist Henri Frugès, who had contacted Le Corbusier in November 1923 after reading *Vers une architecture* and seeing his housing project where the homes complied with the financing stipulations of the Ribot Law. The houses, either detached or semi-detached, have a reinforced-concrete frame and the floors are made of segmented ceramic ribbed vaults, covered in cement cast with the Ingersoll-Rand gun. This small complex is even equipped with its own playing field for the Basque sport pelota.

In 1924, Frugès, an intrepid man, entrusted Le Corbusier with the construction of a much larger complex on a plot of land in Pessac, on the outskirts of the city of Bordeaux. For Le Corbusier this represented a chance to develop all the house types he had worked on since 1914. The community is actually made up of three distinct complexes of 53 housing units, considerably fewer than the 135 units initially planned.

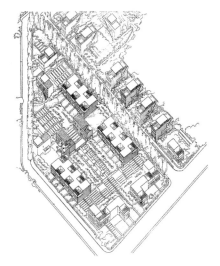

The "Dom-ino" houses, 1925

General axonometric view

It is dominated by a series of taller buildings, "Citrohan" houses, which, owing to their height, are referred to as "skyscrapers." The housing complexes running along the street are based on the "Dom-ino" system, which made it possible to create very different combinations of solids and voids within the same frame. Lastly, the slender vaults of the "Monol" houses were used for a third complex of low housing units.

The project called for the cast cement technique that was deemed suitable for streamlining construction, which proved to be difficult to achieve. The mass production principle was applied in a more effective way in the design of the windows, based on modular elements. The Pessac dwellings, reproduced in 1928 in the brochure *Pour bâtir, standardiser et tayloriser* (For Building, Standardizing and Tailoring), published by Le Corbusier under the auspices of the industrialists' association Le Redressement français, gave for the first time tangible form to the principle of the "machine for living in." The use of colors—ocher, sky blue, sea green—calling to mind the palette of Purist painters, nevertheless lends them a certain three-dimensionality and gives the impression of their being *objets-types* assembled out of doors.

After Pessac, the execution of which turned out to be too costly for Frugès and hastened his bankruptcy, Le Corbusier would continue to develop a type of single-family house based on the contradictory juxtaposition of a load-bearing stonework wall and a metal shell, christened the Loucheur House as a tribute to the minister responsible in 1928 for the massive injection of state subsidies in housing. The occupants of the Pessac dwellings lost no time in altering the Le Corbusier houses, especially after the damage sustained in World War II. They covered the terraces with sloping roofs and partly blocked off the windows lengthwise to create square apertures. The fatalistic Le Corbusier observed: "Life is right and the architect is wrong." In 1980, the complex began to be restored on the initiative of new owners, who were sympathetic to the rigor and elegance of the architect's original solutions.

1925 ▸ "L'Esprit nouveau" Pavilion
destroyed ▸ Cours la Reine, Paris, France

Overall view of an *immeuble-villas*, 1922

The "L'Esprit nouveau" Pavilion was built in just a few weeks at the Exposition internationale des arts décoratifs et industriels modernes in Paris, and inaugurated on July 10, 1925. It served to showcase a condensed version of all the various parts of the Corbusian program, while promoting the eponymous review founded by Jeanneret, Ozenfant and Dermée five years previously, though its end was nigh. Beginning in 1920 *L'Esprit nouveau* introduced its readers to the European cultural scene, and among other things, demanded France's recognition of the USSR. The scientific fields of physics, medicine, experimental psychology and psychoanalysis were addressed on a regular basis in the pages of a publication that was receptive to every kind of novelty. Cinema had pride of place in the columns written by Jean Epstein and Louis Delluc. Le Corbusier did his utmost to determine the look of the magazine, both through his choice of typeface and illustrations for articles—in particular his own—and through the design of advertisements, like those for the "Innovation" trunk. The objects on view in the pavilion offered a representative selection from this world.

The pavilion reproduced in its frontmost part a cell of the *immeuble-villas* shown at the 1922 Salon d'Automne. This theoretical project assembled 200 "Citrohan" houses, whose name conjured up car manufacturing and which illustrated the motto "The house is a machine for living in." The "Citrohan" was a long, rectangular prism open at both ends, containing a two-story living room recalling the studios of Parisian artists, and it would provide many variants. In the *immeuble-villas* each unit had its own garden, like the cells of the Charterhouse of Galluzzo in Val d'Ema, near Florence, where Jeanneret had been impressed in 1911 by the configuration of the monks' two-story dwellings and their gardens, which, together, formed the monastic complex. The building's cells had the advantage of collective utilities, like in American condominiums.

The pavilion included an L-shaped house and the adjoining garden was built around an existing tree. It used a metal structure and filler panels made of compressed straw, on top of which cement was applied with a pneumatic gun. Contrary to the styles

Opposite page:
General view of the pavilion
In the foreground, a sculpture by Jacques Lipchitz; on the right, the glass wall of the "Citrohan" house; at center, the terraced garden; on the left, the wall for the dioramas

The stairway leading to the upper floor

celebrated at the Exposition internationale, the dwelling was furnished with leather armchairs made by the Maple company and bentwood Thonet chairs, the simple design of which was extolled as a virtue in *L'Esprit nouveau*. They were linked to a set of modular "standard racks," Le Corbusier's interpretation of the standardized filing cabinets in modern offices, whose rational and modular qualities he had sung the praises of in his articles. On the walls, painted in the colors of Purist pictures, hung Fernand Léger's *Balustre* (Baluster), Le Corbusier's *Nature morte de l'Esprit nouveau* (Still Life of L'Esprit nouveau) and works by Jacques Lipchitz, Juan Gris and Amédée Ozenfant. Among the objects on display there was an "Innovation" toilet case.

Behind this luminous, truly great architectural manifesto, a darkened room housed urban-planning studies in the form of dioramas of the "Contemporary City" and the Plan Voisin, conceived on this occasion for the center of Paris. His city-planning projects would fall under two major categories: the theoretical and general projects, with no explicit site, and those—commissioned or otherwise—designed for specific locations. The pavilion's dioramas belonged to both categories.

The "Contemporary City for Three Million Inhabitants" of 1922 stood in the tradition of such Utopian projects as Tony Garnier's "Cité industrielle," with which Le Corbusier had been familiar. Its "tidy" structure contrasted with "disorderly" cities. By applying principles worked out in Germany prior to 1914, Le Corbusier devised a city whose business district was crowned with glass skyscrapers. Around the center, featuring a futuristic train station and airport and crisscrossed by a network of freeways, the residential neighborhoods took on the form of "indents," like the broken rows of building alignments designed by the French urbanist Eugène Hénard. Le Corbusier thus demonstrated his ability to emulate and go beyond previous accomplishments.

In 1925 the Plan Voisin, funded by the automobile and aircraft manufacturer Gabriel Voisin after being rejected by Citroën and Peugeot, applied this principle to the very center of Paris, causing unprecedented outrage. His proposal was received by the

press as an "Americanization" of Paris and, paradoxically, spread Le Corbusier's popularity well beyond elite circles. Henceforth his strategy entailed first influencing public opinion in order to win over the decisionmakers. The old quarters of central Paris were to be replaced by office skyscrapers and a "great throughfare," in the shape of a freeway, was to cut through the city. Le Corbusier refused to renew the winding "donkey path" of the medieval city and proffered as a paradigm for the modern city respiratory and circulatory systems, which he wrote about in *Urbanisme*. He had no intention of "carrying on the tradition" of Paris by retaining its historic fabric, but rather by having the new buildings enter into a dialogue with a number of the city's landmarks, such as Notre Dame, the Arc de Triomphe and the Eiffel Tower, which capture the "spirit of Paris," just as his skyscrapers might have done. There was no dearth of political emphasis in this project. As a critic of popular Paris, which he saw as a "dangerous magma of hordes, piled on top of each other, dashing around and appendage-like, a secular encampment of gypsies from all the world's great roads," Le Corbusier proposed an overall "ordering" of the city, a revised version of which would be presented in the "Les Temps nouveaux" Pavilion at the 1937 Exposition universelle in Paris.

The "L'Esprit nouveau" Pavilion was destroyed in 1926, and Le Corbusier failed to find a patron to finance its reassembly. In 1977 at Bologna's convention center, the pavilion was reconstructed in concrete, instead of the original wood frame, by José Oubrerie and Giuliano Gresleri.

Robert Bonfils, poster for the Exposition internationale, Paris, 1925

1926–1927 · Weissenhofsiedlung
Bruckmannweg, Rathenaustraße, Stuttgart, Germany

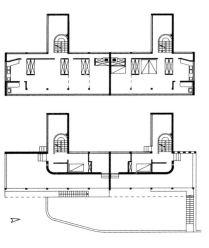

Plan of the ground floor and first floor of the semi-detached house
Left: daytime configuration; right: nighttime configuration

In Stuttgart Le Corbusier's ideas came up against those of his European counterparts at the exhibition organized in 1927 by the Deutsche Werkbund, which was to prove extremely influential for years to come. This organization, which was concerned with improving the relationship between art and industry, built for the exhibition "Die Wohnung" (The Dwelling), an experimental *Siedlung*, or housing complex, on the slopes of the Weissenhof. Ludwig Mies van der Rohe worked on the master plan, and the leading lights of modern German architecture—ranging from Walter Gropius and the Taut brothers to Hans Scharoun and Peter Behrens—were invited to design buildings for it. Josef Frank of Vienna, the Dutchmen Mart Stam and J.J.P. Oud and the Belgian Victor Bourgeois also took part in an operation that was fiercely opposed by the public and conservative critics alike, who saw in it a sort of "Arab village," running quite counter to all German building traditions.

Le Corbusier and Pierre Jeanneret built both a "Citrohan" house and a semi-detached house, in which they experimented with solutions for low-cost housing. They entrusted Alfred Roth with supervising the construction work and selecting the color scheme. The Stuttgart "Citrohan" house, figurehead of the *Siedlung*, is the most elaborate dwelling type developed by Le Corbusier since 1920. The positioning of the windows is an especially innovative solution and makes it possible to gauge the height of each floor, owing to the pilotis in the rear gable, and to imagine the uses to which the rooms could be put, thanks to the glazed areas at the front and the windows with their varying proportions.

The semi-detached house brings together two distinct, symmetrical dwellings that are joined by a row of pilotis and a lengthwise window the size of the building. Diametrically opposed to the wide-open spaces of the "Citrohan" house and many other *Siedlung* units, it represents an experimental arrangement that introduces various daytime and nighttime uses. The living rooms are turned into dormitories by night and the Spartan economy of the nocturnal versions, whose bedrooms are not much larger than railway sleeping-car cubicles, attracted many a sarcastic comment. To present the Stuttgart houses, which were admired by many visitors, including the Russian artist Kasimir Malevich, Le Corbusier wrote one of his most influential manifestoes, in which he outlined "the five points of a new architecture."

The five points stem from the use of a reinforced-concrete frame, permitting a wholesome "liberation." The "paralyzed" plan of stone houses and their restricted facades became "free," usable surfaces were increased as a result of the pilotis and the roof terrace and the ribbon window made it possible to flood the interiors with light. With his new buzzwords and buildings, in ten years, Le Corbusier had radically redefined the word "house," after Adolf Loos in Vienna had called into question the common notion of an abode as early as 1914. The "machine for living in," whose advent Le Corbusier announced, nevertheless assumed many faces, reacting to the requirements of each site and allowing for different uses, but in every instance encouraging the free movement of occupants and visitors and bathing them in an intense light.

Opposite page:
The semi-detached house, 1927

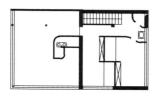

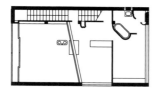

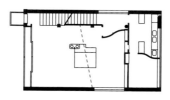

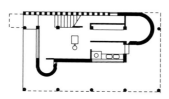

Plan of the different floors of the "Citrohan" house

Top to bottom: terrace; mezzanine; main floor; lower floor with pilotis

The success of the Stuttgart show, after Le Corbusier's failure in the League of Nations competition, led to the founding of the Congrès internationaux d'architecture moderne (CIAM), which whirred into action in the summer of 1928 at La Sarraz Castle near Lausanne. Le Corbusier would play a leading role in the first convention and his ideas would have a powerful impact on the CIAMs in Frankfurt (1929), Brussels (1930), Athens (1933) and Paris (1937), which gave direction to the going collective—and contradictory—thinking about the low-cost dwelling and the functional city.

Above:
General view of the two houses, 1927

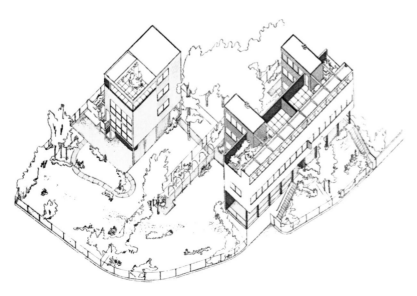

Left:
Axonometric view of the two houses

1926–1928 ▸ Villa Stein-de Monzie

Rue du Professeur Victor-Pauchet, Vaucresson, France

Opposite page:
Garage door and front door

The gallery on the upper floor and a view across to the "large living room"

Villa viewed from the garden

By 1926, Le Corbusier had achieved fame and success, which led him to receive commissions for large houses in posh Paris suburbs—not all of which were actually built. The most impressive and costly of these was the Villa "Les Terrasses" in Garches, on a plot of land that is today part of Vaucresson. It was designed for Michael Stein, brother of the writer Gertrude Stein, his wife, Sarah, and Gabrielle de Monzie, divorced wife of the radical socialist minister Anatole de Monzie, a faithful backer of Le Corbusier, who had enabled the construction of the "L'Esprit nouveau" Pavilion in 1925. The luxury of its rooms would bother the critics, who subscribed to the social dimension of modern architecture.

The facade of this house, set within a parallelepiped, is flat and governed by a regulating plan based on the golden section, which determines the proportions and positioning of the windows. Through its transparency, the garden façade, on the other hand, reveals the complex interplay of the indoor volumes and the walk linking the terraces to one another and to the garden, with access via an outside stairwell. The English architectural critic Colin Rowe has compared the geometric grid that underpins the plan of the house—consisting of alternating broad and narrow fields—to that of Palladio's Villa Malcontenta and has detected hidden parallels that abound in Le Corbusier's oeuvre. Like Robert Slutzky, Rowe thought he recognized in the villa's cylindrical stairwells and curved partitions—which Le Corbusier regarded as "compressed organs"—the *objets-types* featuring in Le Corbusier's Purist paintings, such as *Nature morte à la pile d'assiettes* (Still Life with a Pile of Plates) of 1920. The house may thus be described as a three-dimensionally rendered picture, if you will.

View from the street
Left: Le Corbusier's Voisin C12 car

The vertical arrangement of the rooms is clear and logical. The ground floor houses the garage and the utility areas around a large hall providing access to the upper floor via two staircases, the position of which would be changed throughout the planning phase. The main entrance is fitted with a cantilevered awning, balanced symmetrically by the tradesmen's entrance with a balcony over it. The second floor houses the reception rooms and the kitchen, shared by the Steins and Gabrielle de Monzie. The dining room is separated by a curved partition from the living room, which, with its gallery leading to the entrance hall, opens onto the garden with a large, sheltered terrace. The third floor, which accommodates the bedrooms, is where the separation of both households is most notable, in the form of two distinct apartments, the arrangement of whose communicating bedrooms and their adjoining rooms reveals Le Corbusier as a skilled designer of domestic space and recalls the houses of 18th-century French architects, such as Jacques-François Blondel.

The top floor is given over almost completely to large roof terraces, the smaller of which is reached by way of a rectangular window looking onto the street, the larger of

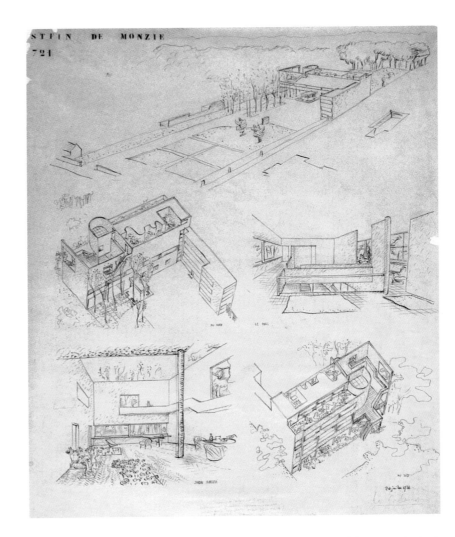

Right:
Sketches, July 1926

Below:
Plan of the first floor

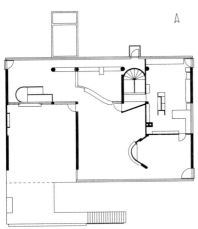

which overlooks the garden and is reached by a stairway located between the bedrooms. The design of the terraces recalls the ocean liners celebrated in *L'Esprit nouveau*. In the film *L'Architecture d'aujourd'hui* (Architecture of Today), which Pierre Chenal made about Le Corbusier in 1930, the architect played himself, arriving at the villa by way of the gravel drive in his Voisin car, thus explicitly linking machine and dwelling. When he revisited the villa in 1959, he saw in it an "exquisite apparition" in which "poetry, technology, biology [and] a human scale" are united.

1928–1931 ▸ Villa Savoye
Rue de Villiers, Poissy, France

Le Corbusier beside the maquette of the villa at the Museum of Modern Art, New York, 1935

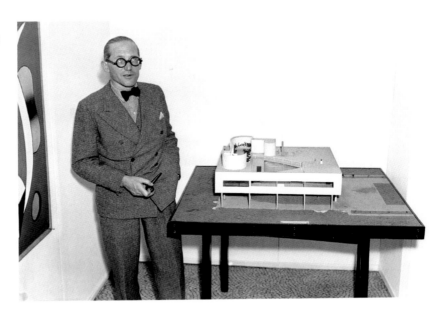

General view

Two years after the Villa Stein-de Monzie was built, the cycle of Purist houses ended with the spectacular weekend home of the insurance underwriter Pierre Savoye in Poissy, called "Les Heures claires" (The Bright Hours), for which Le Corbusier had an extremely generous budget. On a large, wooded site overlooking the Seine valley, it is a perfect example of the free use of the "five points" formulated by the architect in 1927.

Austerely functional on the outside, its volume is supported by pilotis above a large expanse of lawn. Access for cars could not be more direct, for they are parked between the pilotis, beneath the house. The curve of this trajectory is echoed in the semicircular form of the glass wall of the entrance. The servants' bedrooms and the garage are wedged behind this functional access, which seems to reverse the shape of the entrance courtyards of Parisian mansions. Once through the glass wall, visitors have two access options: a stairway and a ramp, which offers the original spatial experience peculiar to the house. In Le Corbusier's eyes, the stairway "separates" whereas the ramp "links." The latter stretches from the lawn to the sky, like a majestic "architectural promenade," extending from the entrance through the apartment on the second floor to the roof terrace.

Within the prism of the square plan the dwelling is arranged, after lengthy studies, in the form of an L that cleanly separates the public areas from the bedrooms. The living room may be regarded as the covered part of a large reception area, two-thirds of which is a patio opening onto the landscape through a continual lengthwise window between interior and exterior that seems to be nothing more than a light diaphragm. Access to the three bedrooms is via corridors isolating the main bathroom. A sinuous

Opposite page:
The outdoor ramp leading to the roof

General view

screen, like certain figures in Purist paintings, wraps around the outdoor room situated on the roof.

This unique building, some of whose features recall the bridges and decks of a ship, is similar to a machine; it also bears a resemblance to the hanging gardens of the Charterhouse of Galluzzo in Val d'Ema, while the arrangement of bedrooms and their annexes—bathrooms and closets—bring to mind grand Parisian mansions of the 18th century. Occupants of these premises are promised sensual delights: the large window in the living room slides open to create a continuity between patio and interior. The luminous bathroom with its top lighting encourages repose. Le Corbusier's spatial experiments are inextricably linked with certain architectural traditions of the past. Yet, they also incorporate the prosaic materials of whitewashed houses in Paris suburbs and components like steel window frames typical of small factories. His houses, therefore, contrast both with dressed stone mansions and with burrstone suburban homes. The concierge's lodge, in striking contrast with the luxury of the villa, is located at the entrance and bears witness to Le Corbusier's investigation of low-cost housing.

In 1930, when he cast a retrospective eye over the houses he had built over the previous ten years, Le Corbusier singled out "four compositions." He contrasted the

Top:
The kitchen

Bottom:
Plans of the ground floor and upper floor

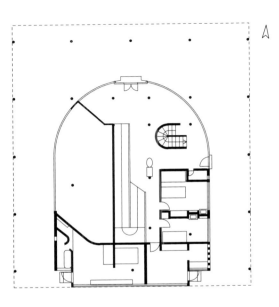

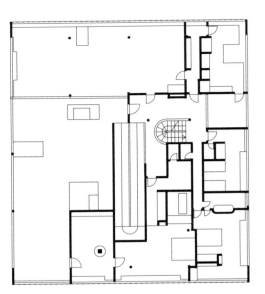

The bathroom with molten glass tiling

The stairway and glass wall on the ground floor

'somewhat facile, picturesque, hectic genre" of the Villa La Roche with the "very difficult" "Citrohan" house's prism, which led, on the other hand, to the "spiritual satisfaction" and the "very easy, practical, combinable" genre of all the "Dom-ino" types. The synthesis of all this is the Villa Savoye, illustrating a "very generous" type, 'on the outside [of which] is asserted an architectural will [and] on the inside every kind of functional need is met." The Villa Savoye was not often occupied by its owners, but remains like a manifesto, which, in 1965, would be the first of Le Corbusier's buildings to become a listed historic edifice in France during his lifetime. Le Corbusier died before restoration work on it started—he had been working on the plans from 1960 onward, and would have changed it considerably.

The living room and the terrace
The entire large glass partition is a sliding door.

1928–1936 ▸ Centrosoyus Building

Ulitsa Miasnitskaya, Moscow, Russia

Facade on rue Miasnitskaya

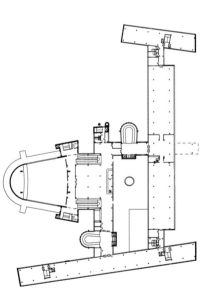

Plan of the stalls in the auditorium and the offices on the same level

Opposite page:
Facade on Novomiasnitskaya Street; on the left, the club room on pilotis

With the League of Nations competition, Le Corbusier ushered in a series of projects for large edifices, shattering the image of the monumental building. He explored several ways of articulating repetitive features, like offices, with one-off elements, such as auditoria and lobbies. As a keen observer of the most diverse reform movements, he pounced on every opportunity he was given to build large edifices and complexes that would embody his radical principles. The largest of these was the Centrosoyus Building, headquarters of Soviet cooperatives, for which he clinched the commission in 1928, after a triumphal visit to Moscow. His admiration for avant-garde architects and the commitment of then Centrosoyus president, Isidore Liubimov, meant that he took first place in the international competition.

The site where it was to be built was located on Miasnitskaya Street, one of Moscow's historic radial roads. For this building, with its concrete frame, he devised an air-conditioning system that was well ahead of its time, combining a "neutralizing wall," consisting of two glass partitions separated by a vacuum, with the "exact respiration" system, which was intended to carry warm air to every room. As the system was too costly, it was swiftly abandoned.

He designed his project with traffic circulation in mind, using spiral ramps, which were to allow up to 2,500 employees to reach the sixth floor. In *Précisions* of 1930, he singled out "two tempos" in the building: "The first a disorderly inflow [of employees], over a vast horizontal expanse at ground level: this is a lake; the second, a stable, motionless work protected from noise and coming and going, everyone at their own place and supervisable: the offices. [Circulation] rivers lead to it, the means of communication . . . *Architecture is circulation*. Think about it; it condemns academic methods and sanctifies the piloti principle."

The layout and assembly of office units were the result of a novel change in his approach to the design, described by Le Corbusier thus: "I am designing the first central block of offices with vertical subdivisions for perfect illumination. This office unit includes large common work rooms and is fitted with an expanse of glass on both sides . . . I am also sketching out the other two office units: an expanse of glass on one side, a mixed wall (stone and glass) forming the corridors. The dimension of these three prisms is essential to the architectural composition; they are arranged plan- and section-wise in such a way as to afford views, here from above, there in a sunken area. The central unit is a floor lower than the two lateral units; this is important. Everything is in mid-air, on stilts, detached."

The critics did not mince their words over the building. Hannes Meyer called it an "orgy of glass and concrete" and conservative Russian architects referred to it as an "alien building." It was completed, after many complications, in 1936, at a time when the Stalinist ice age was beginning to set in, and its most ardent champion then was the Constructivist Aleksandr Vesnin, who would see in it "the best building constructed in Moscow for a century." It was used as the People's Commissariat for Light Industry, and today houses the Goskomstat, Russia's State Office of Statistics.

1929–1933 ▸ Cité de refuge
Rue Cantagrel, Paris, France

Opposite page:

The entrance portico on rue Cantagrel
The present facade is tectonically much more expressive than the original all-glass plan.

Below:

Plan of the ground floor
The reception area is round and the refectories are located in the extended wing.

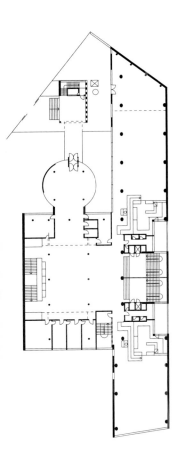

The Cité de refuge was the third project designed by Le Corbusier for the Salvation Army, after the Palais du peuple (People's Palace), built on rue des Cordelières in 1926–27, and the floating refuge ("asile flottant"), a large concrete barge converted into a dormitory for vagrants in 1929–30. Thanks to the generosity of 20,000 donors and Princess Winaretta Polignac-Singer, the shelter was built to house between 500 and 600 homeless Parisians. The incorporation of a huge volume within the fabric of a Paris suburb called for lengthy deliberations before the definitive solution could be found, one separating shared utilities located on the ground floor on rue Cantagrel from the glazed prism of the dormitories, extended by a secondary wing on rue du Chevaleret.

The building's various components bear witness to Le Corbusier's interest, as expressed in *Vers une architecture* (*Towards a New Architecture*, 1927) of 1923, in the design of ocean liners. The sequence of large ground-floor rooms, from the entrance to the reception rotunda, wrapped in slabs of glass, reproduces the series of lounges and smoking rooms in ships. The upper floors, like ship decks, and the overall look of the building, surmounted by superstructures recalling footbridges and gangways, has a ship-like quality. On each level, the series of modular dormitories imitates the monotonous repetition of ships' cabins. And the triplex apartment reserved on the uppermost levels for the building's donor bears a striking resemblance to an admiral's command post.

From the ship, the Cité de refuge also borrows watertightness. It implements the principle of "exact respiration" abandoned in Moscow. Sheaths are meant "hygienically" to ventilate and heat the corridors, dormitories and individual rooms of residents through separate ventilation systems. But the absence of any cooling system in summer, and the impossibility of opening the fixed windows on the south façade, would doom these measures to failure. Since the early 1930s, the Salvation Army clashed with Le Corbusier, who wrote in a letter to Princess Polignac that "persons with their own agendas are getting excited and arguing in a perpetual state of alternating psychological and physical reactions" and that, for his own part, "he felt obliged not to take that into account and to pursue his positive, scientific investigations in peace."

Not far from the Gare d'Austerlitz, the Cité de refuge was severely damaged by bombing in World War II. The completely destroyed facade was rebuilt and transformed by the addition of a *brise-soleil*, or sun screen, designed by Le Corbusier and Pierre Jeanneret, who, after their parting of ways in 1940, collaborated again on this one project.

1931–1934 ▸ Residential Building at Porte Molitor

Rue Nungesser-et-Coli, Paris, France

The building seen from the Jean-Bouin stadium

To erect this building between party walls, on Paris's outermost city limits, Le Corbusier had to abandon one of his *immeuble-villas*, which would have occupied the entire block. Commissioned by the Paris-Parc des Princes real-estate company (Société immobilière de Paris-Parc des Princes) run by the building contractors Kouznetzoff et Noble, he designed an apartment building whose individual units were to be sold. In a neighborhood surrounded by sports facilities that had taken the place of fortifications leveled in 1919, the buildings on rue Nungesser-et-Coli form a long facade facing east towards Paris. Rue de la Tourelle, on the other hand, belongs to the suburb of Boulogne.

The building stands out from the others, such as the adjacent Michel Roux-Spitz structure, on account of its striking metal and glass façade. To begin with, Le Corbusier envisaged using a steel frame, which was swiftly replaced by a cheaper concrete structure. On a site measuring 12 x 25 meters, an axial row of uprights afforded the free arrangement of walls. The projections over the street, which comply with the facade regulations as outlined in Paris's building code of 1902, were made smaller and the building itself squeezed into a constricting shell.

Despite these restrictions, Le Corbusier nevertheless decided to produce "model apartments under the conditions of La Ville radieuse." The ground floor accommodates the lobby, the maids' rooms and a curved entrance to the underground garage. The apartments, on six floors, are arranged in clusters of two and three units, all adaptable to the specific requests of prospective owners. The rooms are configured in a fluid manner, and look onto a small service courtyard and a main courtyard. A facade comprises wired glass, Nevada glass bricks and transparent windows in a steel frame, which admits natural light on each floor.

On the seventh floor, Le Corbusier installed his own apartment, with access via the building's freight elevator, built beneath semicircular vaults, making the best possible use of the allotted space. The living rooms, on the rue de la Tourelle side, are bathed in evening light; in this sequence of rooms the bathrooms merge with the bedrooms. Charlotte Perriand decisively contributed to the design of the kitchen furnishings. Wide pivoting doors lead to the studio, located beneath the largest of the vaults, housing an office nook and a maid's room. Like "rough, clean skin," in Le Corbusier's eyes, the party wall stones lend an irregular backdrop to the room. The wall—an "everyday friend"—enters into a dialogue with the architect's unfinished artistic works. The terrace is accessible via a spiral staircase.

In 1934, Le Corbusier set up home in a place dotted with lyrical objects, but things that Yvonne Gallis found were never "feminine enough." In 1935, gallery owner Louis Carré presented a show of "primitive art" in the studio. A plaster cast of the Greek figure Le Corbusier painted in his Moscophore rubbed shoulders with a piece of Peruvian pottery, a bronze sculpture from Benin and a tapestry by Fernand Léger, illustrating "modern sensibility with an eye on the past, exoticism and the present." This would be the sole public event held in the architect's private sanctuary, which thereafter was to be seen by the public only in photographs.

Opposite page:
View into the apartment
On the left, the spiral staircase leading to the terrace

The studio with its wall of undressed brick and stonework

Left:
The porch and its awning on the roof terrace

Below left:
The breakfast nook with a view over Paris

Plan of the seventh floor
Rue Nungesser-et-Coli is at the top of the drawing

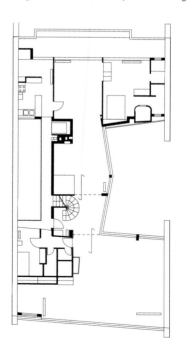

1946–1952 ▸ Unité d'habitation
Boulevard Michelet, Marseilles, France

Opposite page:
The roof terrace
In the foreground, the nursery school; in the
background, the gymnasium

Overall view

The Unité d'habitation in Marseilles was the first commission granted to him by the French State. In order to provide accommodation for those who had lost their homes in the war, he applied a principle that went back to the *immeuble-villas* and the indents of 1922. In Moscow, in 1930, he had noted that Moisei Ginsburg and his Constructivist friends had used his ideas in the Narkomfin communal house, by equipping it with "shared utilities." He took back to Paris the plans for a building that owes a great deal to his own designs. In the 1930s, a double movement gave rise to the notion of the "standard size housing unit." On the one hand, the Clarté Building erected in Geneva in 1930–32 with a metal frame was his first double-height housing complex. On the other hand, he introduced into the "cusps" the continuous horizontal circulations of the Narkomfin Building and began to break them up into separate buildings in his various urban plans. Worked out during the war in *La Maison des hommes* (The House of Man) of 1942, the autonomous "housing unit" principle was used in the reconstruction plan for Saint-Dié of 1944, in which the inhabitants were brought together in six of these buildings.

The Marseilles project went through a difficult gestation period. Commissioned by Raoul Dautry, then Minister of Reconstruction and City Planning, it would be completed thanks to the determination of his successor, Eugène Claudius-Petit, despite the campaign launched against it by conservative architects and unadventurous health experts. After a damning expert's report predicting the development of mental illness among future occupants, a national controversy sprang up and the people of Marseilles nicknamed the building in their local dialect the "Maison du Fada" (the madhouse).

Designed as a "vertical garden city," the complex was conceived for four different sites before ending up on boulevard Michelet, in one of Marseilles's most "beautiful districts." Supported by stout pilotis containing fluid systems, a reinforced-concrete frame, like a "bottlerack," accommodates the "bottles" that form the 337 apartments, whose individual façades, protected by *brise-soleil*, were prefabricated in concrete elements. Running east to west, the units were served by "mid-air streets" designed in 1929, and situated on every third floor. One of these "streets," which was higher and recognizable from the outside by its vertical *brise-soleil*, houses shops and a hotel. Between hills and the sea, with apartment loggias opening on to both, the building's roof terrace accommodates a nursery school and a gymnasium. Anchored in the Mediterranean landscape it also recalls the decks of ocean liners, which Le Corbusier had celebrated for 30 years.

Slowed up by budgetary problems, the construction of the building—Le Corbusier's largest to date—would take five years to complete instead of the initially planned twelve months. This was the first building in which the "Modulor" system of proportions worked out by Le Corbusier in 1943 was introduced. The Unité was also a test bench for simple, mass-produced furniture. Jean Prouvé and Charlotte Perriand not only contributed to the housing unit's elegant components, but were also respon-

The service "street" on the seventh floor
A "public promenade" forms an extension to the "street."

The roof terrace and the gymnasium

sible for designing its built-in cupboards and other furnishings. Yet, for Le Corbusier, the Unité would have made most sense as an ensemble of urban dwellings. The failure of his satellite plan for Marseille-Sud, with 23 units (1947–49), and of his proposals for Strasbourg and Meaux denied him the chance to demonstrate this. He had to content himself with making unusual and individual Unités in Nantes-Rezé, Berlin-Charlotten-burg (as part of the 1957 Interbau Fair), Briey-en-Forêt and Firminy-Vert, if at times under trying conditions.

Reconstruction of an apartment with Le Corbusier's suggested standard furnishings
In the foreground, coffee table and chairs by Charlotte Perriand; in the background, table and chairs by Jean Prouvé

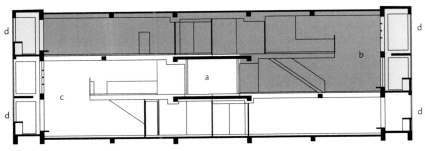

Cross section
a) main corridor
b) "luxury" standard duplex
c) "simple" standard duplex
d) brise-soleils

1951–1952 ▸ "Le Cabanon"

Promenade Le Corbusier, Roquebrune-Cap Martin, France

View of the exterior

In *L'Art décoratif d'aujourd'hui* of 1925, Le Corbusier made a case for the simplicity symbolized by a "naked man." He celebrated the figure of Diogenes and his encounter with geometry, which in his eyes represented the original source of an architecture that eschews the clash of styles. For him, man's invention of the primitive dwelling made him the creator of geometry, as he wrote in 1928 in *Une Maison, un palais*: "Not a piece of wood, in its form and force, not a string, without a specific function. Man is sparing. Won't this hut one day be that Roman Pantheon dedicated to the gods?" His interest in the hut persisted, such as when he proposed, during the war, youth holiday camps with "Murondin" huts covered with rough logs (*rondins*).

Le Corbusier was well acquainted with Roquebrune-Cap Martin, on the French Riviera, from his visits in 1927 to Eileen Gray and Jean Badovici's E 1027 home, where he later painted some controversial frescoes. He worked on the "Roq" project on site in 1948–50 and stayed at the Etoile de Mer restaurant, run by Thomas Rebutato, during the summer of 1949, to design the Bogota plan. Having become a regular at the restaurant, he translated his thoughts into reality by constructing a log cabin using logs only partly stripped of their bark. The dimensions, using the "Modulor" range, were minimized: the structure occupied an area of only 3.66 meters, with a height, from the ground to the top of the lean-to roof, of 2.26 meters.

The rustic building, "drawn on the corner of a table" in 1951, contrasted with the clearly defined white forms of the adjacent E 1027 house, as well as with the five "camping units" made of wooden panels, built by Le Corbusier in 1957 alongside the Etoile de Mer, the realized versions of his ambitious "Rob" project. Le Corbusier worked out the proportions of the *cabanon* based on a composition involving a centripetal spiral, a system so complex that it is virtually unrecognizable owing to the apparent simplicity of the structure. The apertures were kept to a minimum: two square windows, two vertical slits for ventilation and a small window, which casts light onto a low table. The interior comprises an entrance hall and a wash room on one side of the hut and one room containing two single beds, a table and a washbasin on the other. The seating consists of wooden parallelepipeds, like the wall paneling and furniture. With this "humble shack" Le Corbusier plays with the contraction and expansion of space. The framed views of the horizon would seem to belie the compactness of the Spartan furnishings. Even simpler, an adjacent "work shack," measuring 4 x 2 meters, served as the architect's workplace. Just a few yards away the architect would die in the summer of 1965, after having gone for a swim in the ocean.

In his "little studio," a cubic wooden dwelling rising to a height of 2.26 meters, built in his office at no. 35, rue de Sèvres, Le Corbusier settled into the life of a recluse right in the center of Paris. Was it out of longing for the Mediterranean summers that Le Corbusier shut himself away in this "retreat," to escape from background noise and to make sure that visitors remained "brief and to the point"? In any event, at Roquebrune-Cap Martin, some several hundred meters above the cabin, he would build his last abode, the grave where he now lies buried next to his wife, Yvonne Gallis.

Opposite page:
The dining nook
Wooden boxes serve as seats.

1951–1955 · Church of Notre-Dame-du-Haut

Colline de Bourlémont, Ronchamp, France

Aerial view of the church and its environs
In the foreground, the pilgrims' house

The visual revolution of the Ronchamp church astounded Le Corbusier's supporters and followers and is the product of his encounter with ecclesiastical architecture. In the postwar period his projects offered him the opportunity to investigate domestic space. On Bourlémont Hill, the last spur of the Vosges range, rising to 500 meters, he was asked to rebuild the Church of Notre-Dame-du-Haut, a historic place of pilgrimage that had been leveled by bombing during World War II. In spite of his almost congenital mistrust of the Catholic Church, he responded to the demands of the sacred art movement, which advocated the introduction of modern architecture and modern painting in religious buildings. Fathers Couturier and Régamey and the laymen François Mathey and Maurice Jardot managed to persuade him to take on the project.

On his first visit, in 1950, he was won over by a site akin to the Jura peaks he had discovered with L'Eplattenier 40 years earlier. He pounced on the chance to "unite men with the cosmos," like the Indian observatories he had discovered around the same time. His project would thus be "site specific." He learned about its history, reading a book written on the church by canon Belot, and came up with the idea of formulating "a word addressed to the site," something like a "response to the horizons." The terrain and its location were certainly determining factors of the design, but not the only ones. The basic idea went back to the discovery on a Long Island beach of an empty crab's shell, similar to those painted on his canvases in the 1930s, which lent the roof of the chapel, perched on four stout walls, its form.

Based on this initial idea, he designed successive maquettes of wire and wood, on which the final plan of 1952 was modeled. Construction continued until 1954. The shell of the roof is made like an airplane wing with two frames and an envelope; the walls, which are independent and separated from the shell by a narrow slit, are an assemblage of veils and reinforced-concrete pillars, a skeleton on which the inner and outer cladding is fixed. The south wall is both thicker and more tapered than the others, and during the design phase the load-bearing east wall, initially so slender as to resemble a "tent peg," was transformed into a honeycomb church. The floor tiling and altars are made of stone. The chapel's plan, which became increasingly asymmetrical as the planning phase progressed, was governed, inside and out, by the position of the altars. A 17th-century polychrome statue of the Virgin, the sole vestige of the destroyed church, is placed such that it is visible to the congregation, priests and acolytes alike.

Besides the crab's shell, other, disparate images fueled Le Corbusier's inventiveness: modern images, like "ski-jumping" gargoyles protruding from the roof, borrowed from hydroelectric dams, as well as those drawn from his earliest memories. The shafts of light penetrating the side chapels conjure up the *serapeum* in Hadrian's Villa, sketched by Jeanneret in 1911. He described it as a "mysterious hole" where he had "discovered a trick." The surprising *brise lumière* on the south wall, with its niches imbued with a clarity modulated by color, conjures up the walls of the Sidi Brahim Mosque in El Atteuf, which the architect discovered during his visit to the Pentapolis in Algeria's M'zab in 1931. The periscope-like belfries recall the funerary stelae of Ischia.

Opposite page:
View of the south and east facades

65

The interior with a view of the south wall

The south door of enameled steel
Images of the earth and the cosmos. Below left,
the "meander of complications"

The interplay of matter and light introduced at Ronchamp broke with the smooth surfaces and homogeneous clarity of the 1920s. Light and shadow now became instruments for sculpting space. And the facade, the sole virtue of which used to be its "freeness," now makes it possible to apply these instruments, owing to the thickness of the wall. Under this dramatic lighting, the white, grainy concrete of the walls and the rough-cast concrete of the roof replace the smooth, homogeneous facades of the "machines for living in" by bearing the unmistakable mark of human labor. In 1954, Le Corbusier asked Edgar Varèse, in vain, to compose a suitable piece of music for the building.

The north facade

Plan

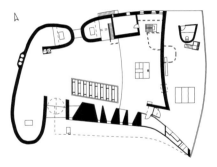

1951–1955 ▸ Jaoul Houses

Rue de Longchamp, Neuilly-sur-Seine, France

View of house A from house B

The Jaoul Houses were finished in 1955, and are among Le Corbusier's studies and designs that once and for all break with his white villas of the 1920s. The stone basement of the Loucheur House of 1928, the brickwork and stonework of the villa built for Hélène de Mandrot in Le Pradet near Toulon of 1931 and, lastly, the one-floor "little weekend house" constructed in La Celle-Saint-Cloud in 1935, with open stonework and slender concrete vaults, represent the milestones of this development. Forming a counterpoint to the sculptural inventiveness in Ronchamp, these attest to Le Corbusier's ability to reinvent himself.

In 1937, he had already designed a weekend home for the aluminum manufacturer André Jaoul, whom he had met on his trip to the United States in 1935. Now he was engaged in constructing, in a suburb of Paris, a house for Jaoul, his wife Suzanne and their children, and another for his son Michel and his family. The two homes were set on one and the same plinth containing the garage and accessible via a single ramp. The first is parallel to the street and the second, set back from it at right angles. They share a courtyard on to which the kitchens open up, each with its own garden.

The industrial, open-jointed brick façades, punctuated with windows of widely varying shapes and sizes, are broken up by rough horizontal concrete bands. Surmounting the thick walls, slender vaults made of terracotta tiles, their backs filled with concrete, conjure up those Catalan roofs discovered by the architect in Spain before the war, as well as houses in the Cyclades. These elements, combined with the village atmosphere of the two homes, would lead the Scottish architect James Stirling to see a similarity between them and farms in Provence, or traditional houses in India. Comparing, item by item, their almost primitive ruralness with the urban character of the Villa Stein-de Monzie, he noted in 1955 that "frequently accused of being 'internationalist,' Le Corbusier is actually the most regionalist of all architects."

The difference between the Jaoul Houses and the Purist villas becomes even more pronounced when one ventures across the threshold. The volume of the ground floor of each house is punctuated by autonomous sculptural elements such as the staircase and the fireplace. Partition walls divide the space without enclosing it, lending it a fluidity that the austere exterior conceals. In the large two-story living room, the kitchen resembles a narrow cube, like railway kitchens, and both homes conjure up trains by the curve of their ceilings. The massive fireplace is punctuated with niches and shelves, recalling the ubiquitous stove so familiar in eastern European households.

But it is above all in the play of light that Le Corbusier broke with the prewar houses in this "habitable volume, full of possibilities." Light is admitted from all sides of the rooms, through wide windows and narrow slits, thus engendering an interior of subtle nuances, but whose plywood paneling lend it a harmonious character. In this way several activities were possible in one and the same room, where the lighting varied depending on the weather and the time of day.

The windows range from small ones, giving a concentrated, local light, to large ones, stretching from floor to ceiling, but interrupted by wooden panels and ribbands,

Opposite page:
Interior of house A

Above:
Interior of house A

Right:
Stairs in house B

Plan of the ground floor of houses A (parallel to the street) and B (at right angles to the street)

Living room in house B

Below:
Exterior of house B

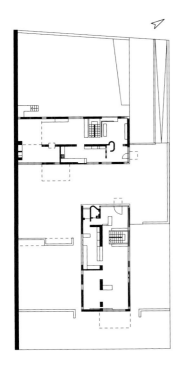

which to a certain extent allow the frames to be varied according to the intended use of each space. The windows form part of a complex interplay with the solid expanses of the walls and the overall geometry of the architectural ensemble and produce a sculptural effect as prescribed by the "Modulor" system of proportions.

The walls, either colored or fitted with paneling, and the warm hue of the bricks represented a new range of materials, used by Le Corbusier at the same time in the Sarabhai House in Ahmedabad, India. The Jaoul Houses seem at first glance to be the very opposite of the Purist villas, while establishing a link with 18th-century apartment blocks in Paris. Adjacent to the bedrooms are a linen room, storage areas, a bathroom with toilet and even an oratory, like in the plans of early Parisian mansions. With the terrace, which opens on to the city, these rooms are a perfect place to relax.

If, as Stirling once so aptly noted, the Jaoul Houses are so comfortable that they run counter to the very idea of the "machine for living in," and "appeal to everyone," this is undoubtedly because they are the work of an architect who had gained much experience over a 30-year period. The Bohemian ready to sacrifice comfort gave way to a more sensual architect, one more attentive to the demands of domestic life, but no less imaginative.

1951–1956 ▸ Shodhan House

Kharawala Road, Ahmedabad, Gujerat, India

Ground-floor living room

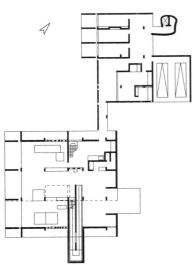

Plan of the ground floor

Opposite page:
Outside view

The fate of the three houses that Le Corbusier designed for influential families in Ahmedabad, capital of the Indian state of Gujerat and a hub of the textile industry, were very different. The house built for Manorama Sarabhai echoes the Jaoul Houses with its brick walls and concrete vaults. The villa designed for the city's mayor, Chinubhai Chimanbhai, was never built. And the plans for the third home, commissioned initially by Surottam Hutheesing, secretary general of the Millowners'—or Textile Manufacturers'—Association and a cousin of the mayor, were bought by his colleague Shyamubhai Shodhan, who had it built on another site.

The initial plan, devised for the hedonistic life-style of Hutheesing, a fun-loving bachelor who wished to have a place for receptions and parties, was adapted without much trouble to the specific needs of Shodhan's family of four children. The overall proportions of the house and its parasol roof principle recall Moghul constructions and, in particular, the Diwan-i-Khas in Fatehpur Sikri. In his sketchbooks, didn't Le Corbusier reproduce numerous of these airy homes shown in Indian miniatures?

The house may be seen as taking up several of the themes of Le Corbusier's earlier residential architecture. The cut of its roof, borne on visible pillars, resembles that of the Villa Baizeau in Carthage, but the ramp that leads to the upper floors recalls the ramp in the Villa Savoye, which, according to *Œuvre complète* of Le Corbusier, it reproduces "in the tropical, Indian manner." The L-shaped configuration of the two upper floors calls to mind the final plan for the Villa Meyer of 1926, which is also arranged around an empty space. But the clever gradation of light and shadow offered by the variously sized windows and the *brise-soleil* create a spectacular visual interplay of forms that is not found in the houses of the 1920s.

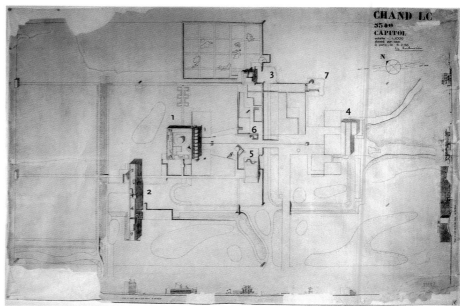

1951–1955 ▸ High Court

Sector 1 ▸ Chandigarh, Punjab, India

Above:
Facade of the High Court looking towards the Capitol

Opposite page:
Overall plan of the Capitol
1) Assembly
2) Secretariate
3) Governor's Palace (not built)
4) High Court
5) "Moat of Contemplation"
6) Pools of water
7) The sculpture the *Open Hand*

Le Corbusier was anything but Jawaharlal Nehru's first choice to design the Punjab's new administrative capital, necessitated by the secession of Pakistan, which had robbed the state of Punjab of its historic capital, Lahore. The master plan of Chandigarh—so named as a tribute to the deity Chandi—was first entrusted to the New York city planner Albert Mayer, who had spent the war in India, while Polish-born architect Matthew Nowicki was to design the city center. After the latter was killed in a plane crash, Le Corbusier was recruited in 1950 to complete the project for a capital that Nehru was keen to have "symbolic of the freedom of India, unfettered by the traditions of the past . . . an expression of the nation's faith in its future."

In his master plan, Le Corbusier retained the principle of neighborhood units proposed by Mayer, but he adjusted the hierarchy of the thoroughfares according to the "7V" principle, which took into account the speed and links permitted by them, from arterial roads (V1) to footpaths (V7).

For the first time, Le Corbusier designed a city center housing the government headquarters as opposed to a business district, which was always the focal point of his earlier plans. It was an extremely innovative plan of large, freestanding buildings "reacting poetically" to each other, their axes lending structure to the open spaces. The center was to have been "crowned" by the Governor's Palace, but this idea was scrapped after three successive proposals had been made. With the High Court Le Corbusier was finally able to realize his basic idea.

The building forms the southeast cornerstone of the Capitol. Like a colossal "parasol and umbrella," it combines beneath its protective roofing, which is 55 in. thick, two clearly separated blocks with access from the rear: the three-story courtroom of the Chief Justice in the High Court and a row of eight smaller courts and offices on two stories. Three monumental pillars from floor to roof separate the two blocks, which the architect described to the Indian engineer P. L. Varma in this way: "Do you know what the High Court is about? Let me tell you, Varma, it's about majesty, the power and home of the law." Access to the upper floors is afforded by a ramp, where the architectural walkabout is sheltered by the shade of the portico. The gradual climb up it reveals the vast expanse of the Capitol and the colored concrete volumes of the building and its apertures with their rounded corners in the concrete pillars.

The rooms are shielded from the at times glaring light by a *brise-soleil*, whose design conjure up the joints of a stone wall; they refer to the solutions that Pierre Jeanneret put into practice in his Chandigarh buildings, featuring brick and concrete frames painted white. The discovery of Moghul palaces, like the Red Fort in Delhi, where the air is cooled in shaded places, was a source of inspiration for Le Corbusier's solutions. The acoustics of the rough-cast concrete rooms were improved by fitting the rear wall of each room with an "acoustic tapestry."

1951–1958 ▸ Secretariate
Sector 1 ▸ Chandigarh, Punjab, India

Overall view

Adjacent to the High Court, at the west end of the complex, the long, low-rise Secretariate—254 meters long and 42 meters high—is a striking administrative building that, as Le Corbusier noted in his sketchbooks, accommodates the "cellular industrious mass" of employees. The initial idea was to create an office tower, building the unrealized skyscraper for Algiers. In its final form, the skyscraper was laid on its side, so to speak, without foregoing the expressive strength of the North African project.

Echoing the Marseilles Unité d'habitation, it comprises a sort of "administration unit," consisting of six eight-story buildings that are joined together. The earth removed to create it was used to make a hilly landscape, on which the edifice appears to float. The offices can be reached via two ramps, instead of stairwells. This solution was borrowed from the plan conceived 20 years earlier for the Centrosoyus Building in Moscow. An architectural landscape is created by the roofs, as in Marseilles.

The administrative hierarchy within the building is readily recognizable from the outside. Above the lower floors are the departmental offices, 3.66 meters high, occupying five of the six "blocks." Accessed by way of a central corridor, they are sheltered by a standardized *brise-soleil*, whose main element forms a tall dwarf wall. Offset by the ensemble's axis of symmetry, the "block" of ministries encompasses various high rooms, which, on the Assembly side, are twice the height of the offices. They can be easily identified by their large loggias, which provide a sculptural counterpoint to the serial look of the other offices.

This symphony of facade rhythms is regulated by the "Modulor." The *brise-soleil* is intended to protect the expanse of "undulating" windows of the buildings from the punishing Indian sun. The building's facade thus becomes a kind of wall of framed images, like a page in a book, as if the building were subject to the same laws governing the design of books, which Le Corbusier had written and designed since 1945.

1951–1962 ▸ Assembly

Sector 1 ▸ Chandigarh, Punjab, India

The hypostyle hall

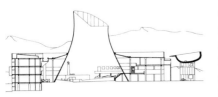

Cross section of the assembly hall

At the northwest tip of the Capitol Le Corbusier erected two buildings designed to house the political and administrative heart of the Indian Punjab—the Secretariate (seven ministries) and the Assembly. When looking at the ensemble from the High Court, the Secretariate serves as a backdrop for the Assembly, the most complex building in Chandigarh. In its design it recalls the Monastery of La Tourette whose courtyard has been filled in and, in its siting on the periphery of the district, an expanded Villa Savoye. The three main components are the portico, facing the rest of the complex, and the two assembly rooms, with their distinctive roofs. These three volumes are surrounded by U-shaped offices.

The forms used have very different origins, and the building seems to reflect Le Corbusier's artistic findings as well as his thoughts on cosmic forces. The revolutionary hyperboloid housing the Lower Chamber derives from the cooling towers studied and drawn in Ahmedabad ca. 1951, but it also recalls the pyramidal smokehouses (*chambres du tué*) in which Jura farmers smoke pork, which had so impressed Jeanneret in his youth. In a more general way, the interplay of this object, its access tower and the pyramid covering the Upper Chamber on the roof calls to mind a strange sun ritual. Le Corbusier declared that "this hat will become a veritable physics laboratory, equipped to ensure the play of light and shadow . . . This cork will be used for solar festivals, reminding man once a year that he is the son of the Sun." If the two odd horns perched atop the hyperboloid evoke the horns of Indian cows that Le Corbusier drew, then the roof landscape recalls the astronomical instruments of the Jantar Mantar, the 18th-century observatory that he had visited in Delhi.

The most majestic entrance to the Assembly, reflected in a large pool of water, creating a kind of virtual cube, is not reached via the footbridge linking the building with the Secretariate, but instead via the large portico opposite the esplanade. The main entrance is fitted with a door made of enameled steel, a gift from France to the Punjab, on which Le Corbusier depicted many of the motifs that then permeated his work, in particular *Le Poème de l'angle droit* (The Poem of the Right Angle) of 1955. Beneath the course of the sun, alongside the tortoise, the bull, the snake, the fish and the "Modulor" man, we see the eagle of Zarathustra. The dazzling brightness outside is followed by the shady "forum," a hypostyle room where a forest of columns determines the basic visual rhythm—punctuated by individual elements like stairways and ramps. The large volume of the Lower Chamber, which is slightly offset, is the "main event," with its unique circular extrados, which let in fresh air and light. The Assembly, which was inaugurated in 1962, has been shared since 1967 by the states of the Punjab and Haryana.

Opposite page:
Overall view

1953–1960 ▸ La Tourette
Monastery ▸ Eveux-sur-l'Arbresle, France

The oratory

Jeanneret was moved by his discovery of the monastic world when he visited the Charterhouse of Galluzzo in Val d'Ema as early as 1907 and Mount Athos in 1911. In a letter to Marguerite Tjader-Harris, he described the "hard and arduous life" of the monks and referred to their asceticism as "heroic." Comforted by the working conditions at Ronchamp, he accepted the commission proposed by Father Couturier to build a Dominican monastery located on the edge of Lyons, on a plot of land purchased by the order during the war. In order to create "a place of meditation, study and prayer for the preaching friars," he visited the Cistercian monastery of Le Thoronet, in the south of France, which deeply impressed him.

His first plans for an open, slightly southward-sloping site, date from 1953 and feature an orthogonal building, whose siting is somewhat awkward. The definitive plan drawn up in 1954 is, on the other hand, more subtle. Its execution would be slow, on account of the Dominicans' limited budget. As in all his large buildings designed since the 1920s, he combined and contrasted two orders of standardized elements: here the monks' cells and the communal areas. In this connection, Le Corbusier was interested in the historical typology of Cistercian monasteries. He did not literally reproduce the cloister with its galleries surrounding the empty central space, the first example of which he saw in Val d'Ema, but reversed the arrangement. The cloister and ambulatory occupy the center of the space, separating the remaining areas of the monastery in the shape of a cross, forming four courtyards. The building does not appear to be firmly anchored in the ground, but somehow attached to the horizontal plane of the overarching roof, and it touches the ground by way of the concrete grid, "as best it can," as Le Corbusier was wont to say.

A U-shaped building houses the monks' cells, which assume the most extreme form of his low-cost spaces designed in the 1920s and modeled on railway sleeping compartments and ship's cabins. The apartments, which are of the same shape as those of the Unités d'habitation, are reduced to their simplest form, their *brise-soleil* actually having been recycled from the Unité in Nante-Rezé. The cells are fitted with a washbasin and Spartan furniture. Access to them is by way of corridors lit by long, narrow windows that lead to the central courtyard. The part of the U that faces south links the refectory with the library, opening inwardly through a wall in which the architect alternated glazed and solid rectangles, which is why it is known as the "Mondrian wall."

The parallelepiped church, an autonomous unit separated by a small interim space from the cells in the U, illustrates a new concept worked out by Le Corbusier—the concept of the "miracle box," a large room in which all sorts of events could be held, and which he tried in vain to execute in Tokyo. Darkness—a new theme—reinforced by the black stone of the floor beneath the altar, is illuminated by an east-facing vertical slit in the wall and a west-facing horizontal slit. In a crypt, adjacent to the main room, the seven altars on which the Dominicans simultaneously celebrate their mass, complying with a rite peculiar to the order (done away with after the Second Vatican

Opposite page:
The monastery in the countryside near Lyons

Above:
The light barrels illuminating the side chapels

Above right:
The side chapels and their seven altars

Opposite page, top left:
Plan of the second floor:
a) Chapter
b) Refectory
c) Office
d) Church
e) Atrium
f) Oratory
g) Vestry
h) Altar
i) Side chapels

Opposite page, top right:
Corridor next to the monks' cells

Opposite page, bottom:
A monk's cell

Council), are enveloped in an undulating wall and lit by "light cannons," which bathe the crypt's colored surfaces in light. The sacristy is located in the "transept" and is lit by seven oblique, haphazardly arranged "light machine guns."

Close to the entry marked by three cylinders is a small chapel surmounted by a concrete pyramid. The galleries intersect in an "atrium" covered by a sloping roof and provide a counterpoint in the form of a rich "architectural promenade," enabling visitors to discover the main volumes of the building and the landscape, above which they seem to float on thin slabs of concrete. The walls of the galleries are punctuated by "undulating" windows, the proportions of the wooden frames of which are determined by the "Modulor" system, that cast ever-changing, linear shadows on the ground. The execution of the project owes much to the man who supervised it, Yannis Xenakis, a young Greek engineer who had fled to Paris as a political refugee. At the same time he was producing his major work *Metastasis*, whose musical sequences are taken up in the "undulating windows" of Ronchamp.

In Le Corbusier's eyes a "labor of love," this "rough-cast concrete monastery" certainly both perplexes and awakens interest. The American architectural historian Vincent Scully compared it with Le Corbusier's villas of the 1920s. He sees in the "Citrohan" house a Greek megaron with four solid walls and a single glazed one, and in the Villa Savoye a "sandwich." For him La Tourette is "a megaron dreaming of turning into a sandwich (or vice versa)." Colin Rowe, on the other hand, noted that "the architect has deliberately focused on translating the academic debate into artistic terms" and that the monastery "is less a church surrounded by dwellings than a domestic theater for ascetic virtuosos, doubling as a gymnasium for the training of spiritual athletes." After the order was forced to abandon its program in La Tourette, the monastery was turned into a cultural center.

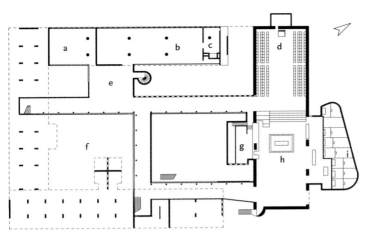

1958 ▸ Philips Pavilion
destroyed ▸ Brussels Exposition universelle, Belgium

A few years after Ronchamp, the pavilion of the Dutch firm Philips at the Brussels Exposition universelle revealed the extent of the upheavals occurring in Le Corbusier's artistic universe. It was the impact made on him by the Ronchamp church that prompted L. C. Kalff, art director at Philips, to entrust Le Corbusier with designing the pavilion. The English composer Benjamin Britten was originally commissioned to write the music to accompany it. But Le Corbusier suggested Edgar Varèse as composer instead, who would contribute to the creation of an ephemeral *Gesamtkunstwerk*, or total work of art.

The early sketches show a building in the shape of a bottle or a "stomach." Entrusted to Yannis Xenakis, who made the design models with piano strings, thread and cigarette paper, it took on a new look. The surfaces bore a pattern of hyperbolic paraboloids, which recalled his score for *Metastasis*, composed in 1954. They were erected as a steel and concrete frame. The steel cables were attached to large concrete supports and clad with prefabricated panels. These cables, used as early as 1937 in the "Les Temps nouveaux" Pavilion at the Paris Exposition internationale, made it possible here to create an utterly new type of volume—a "miracle box" with sinuous outlines.

The pavilion consisted of a large container in which visitors could see images projected on to its walls, accompanied by Varèse's "Electronic Poem" composed for the occasion—a soundtrack played through 425 loudspeakers and 20 amplifiers. The six-minute slide presentation was, according to Le Corbusier, intended to illustrate "in a tumultuous uproar our civilization hell-bent on conquering modern times." The abstract color images of the "Poem" represented for Jean Petit, who put them together, an "ideal imaginative museum" that contradicted the images taken from nature, science and art from around the world, the views of factories, the cliché ideas about the cosmos and many other things, and entered into a dialogue with them. Advanced systems of electronic synchronization of sound and image were installed. But the fear of seeing what the harshness of winter would do to the structure and its electronic equipment led to its being dismantled after the exhibition closed.

Above:
Interior view with purple ambience
The low partition hides the lighting and projection equipment.

Right:
Plan

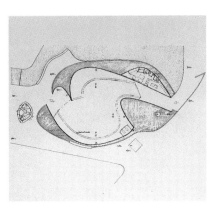

Opposite page:
Overall view

1959 ▸ National Museum of Western Art
Ueno-koen, Taito-ku, Tokyo, Japan

View of the exterior

Opposite page:
Inside the main hall

Plan of the first floor

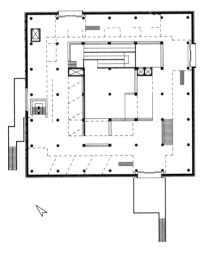

For 30 years, Le Corbusier continued to develop his thoughts on museum architecture, before actually realizing them, in mature form, in Ueno Park, Tokyo, a few hundred yards away from his imposing, indeed forbidding, National Museum built in the 1930s. This building type would seem to have emerged in 1928 in the Mundaneum project, in the form of a tiered pyramid, a ziggurat, which Frank Lloyd Wright would incorporate into his Guggenheim Museum in New York. Later, in 1931, Le Corbusier designed the "museum with unlimited growth," in which the galleries were arranged spiral-like on a single floor, supported by a "forest of pilotis." In this hypothetical design, which he refined time and again, it is possible to see a kind of hypertrophy of the Villa Savoye.

Le Corbusier incorporated a museum into almost all his city-planning projects of the 1930s, from the Zlín Valley to Rio, and made it the object of an effort to build one in Paris, in the form of a "Center of Contemporary Aesthetics," proposed for the city's 1937 Exposition internationale. The museum cropped up again in 1945, in the Saint-Dié plan. Now calibrated to the "Modulor" proportions, it was realized in two versions, one in Ahmedabad (N.C. Mehta Museum of Miniatures, 1952–57) and the other in Chandigarh (Museum and Art Gallery, 1960–65), albeit in a closed, inflexible form that scarcely allows for potential "growth" of the building as the collections grow.

Le Corbusier's fame had reached Japan in the 1920s, and it was in Tokyo that he undertook the most impressive of his three museums. It houses the Matsukata Collection of Impressionist paintings, seized by France in World War II and returned to Japan on the condition that it be presented in a worthy manner. With the help of Kunio Maekawa and Junzo Sakakura, who had worked in Le Corbusier's office and built the Japanese Pavilion for the 1937 Exposition internationale in Paris, he designed an ensemble that encompassed the museum and a "miracle box," which was never realized.

At the entrance of Ueno Park, in the museum's forecourt, stands a bronze cast of Auguste Rodin's *The Thinker*. Above the ground floor the facade comprises concrete panels covered with green pebbles; the ground-floor facade consists of glass. The stairway is located in front of the building, resembling a sculpture. The central area takes the form of a large hall, with a single post supporting its glass roof. The hall is extended by a ramp that provides access to the galleries. As one walks up, it gradually reveals the full extent of the vast space. The galleries, whose muffled atmosphere recalls that of an aquarium, are lit evenly by a complex system that regulates the amount of daylight that is admitted.

Le Corbusier was restricted in each of the museums he built by the constraints of their sites and budgets, and he would never manage to lend form to his idea of a dynamic museum building, which, through its very plan, would demonstrate the evolution of art and the various links between movements and disciplines. He would die before he was able to take the last opportunity offered to him when André Malraux commissioned from him a "Museum of the 20th Century," which was to be situated in the Paris business district of La Défense, but, in a final struggle, the architect unsuccessfully tried to have it moved to the center of the city, on the site of the Grand Palais.

1959–1962 ▸ Carpenter Center for the Visual Arts
Quincy Street, Cambridge, Massachusetts, USA

General view from Prescott Street

Le Corbusier's ideas were, to a large degree, incorporated into the United Nations Headquarters in New York City, that was built by Wallace Harrison and for which Le Corbusier never tired of claiming authorship. Only the Carpenter Center for the Visual Arts can truly be regarded as his own work on United States' soil—an unfair and undeserved state of affairs for an architect who felt drawn to America all his life. As early as 1913, Le Corbusier was fascinated by images of American industry, but on his first trip there, in 1935, he sought in vain support for his ideas on a "cellular reconstruction" of New York and returned to Europe with no new commissions.

He therefore enthusiastically seized the chance offered him in 1959, through Josep Lluís Sert, to construct a building for the arts department at Harvard University. He was well aware that this would be his one and only opportunity to present in the United States a final synthesis of his thoughts and theories on architecture and art. In the heart of the university town of Cambridge, Massachusetts, a stone's throw from the brick buildings of Harvard Yard, between the Neoclassical Fogg Museum and the Faculty Club, the site offered to him lay between Quincy Street and Prescott Street; in no way did it invite monumental designs and at first glance it seemed wholly inadequate to him.

Le Corbusier conceived the Carpenter Center from the very beginning as an "architectural promenade" that would link the two streets and in his studio he developed in paintings ever-changing, undulating forms that were to be incorporated into the building. In an initial plan, designed as a maquette with the young Chilean

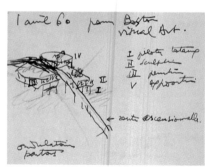

Early sketch of the center, notebook P 60
The promenade-like ramp features in this early drawing.

Opposite page, top:
Inside the studios

Opposite page, bottom:
Plan of the second floor

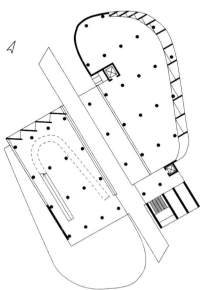

architect Guillermo Jullian de la Fuente, the ramp of the "promenade" was articulated as a spiral. In the final plan it emerged as a thin, S-shaped concrete surface linking the streets, passing through the Center by way of a large porch, from which passersby could get a glimpse of the studios.

The building may be compared to the Millowners' Association building in Ahmedabad, India, an open-plan, single-story structure protected by a *brise-soleil* and entered by way of a sculpture ramp. As in Ahmedabad, albeit in a more demonstrative way, Le Corbusier drew from the whole fund of architectural and artistic themes he had addressed since 1945, rediscovering some of his earliest concepts, such as the "Domino" principle. He thus explored several of the *brise-soleil* solutions formulated since the Algier's skyscraper and, for the plan of both parts of the building, he used a kind of "lung," resembling a model presented in *Urbanisme* (*The City of Tomorrow and Its Planning*, 1929) in 1925.

The execution of the Carpenter Center project was supervised by Sert, who had worked with Le Corbusier from 1928 to 1930 and helped him deal with those detractors who accused him of not using "béton brut," a kind of rough-cast concrete, but "brutal concrete." Many of the building's surfaces were polished to a smooth finish, which prompted the architect to declare that he had found "the key to the solution of reinforced concrete."

Life and Work

Yvonne Gallis, Le Corbusier's wife

Opposite page:
Le Corbusier at the CIAM in Brussels, in front of the plans for the "Ville Radieuse," 1930

1887 ▶ Charles-Edouard Jeanneret is born on October 6 at no. 38, rue de la Serre, in La Chaux-de-Fonds, Switzerland. His father, Georges-Edouard Jeanneret-Gris (1855–1926), is an enameller of watchcases and a mountaineer. His mother, Marie-Charlotte-Amélie Perret (1860–1960), is an amateur pianist.

1902 ▶ He enters the School of Decorative Arts in La Chaux-de-Fonds, taking classes in engraving and carving.

1905 ▶ He attends the advanced course introduced by Charles L'Eplattenier (1874–1946).

1906 ▶ With René Chapallaz (1881–1976) he builds the Fallet House, La Chaux-de-Fonds, followed by the Jacquemet and Stotzer Villas in the same town, which are both finished in 1908.

1907 ▶ After completing his studies, he travels to Italy with the sculptor Léon Perrin (1886–1978). Thereafter, he spends six months in Vienna.

1908 ▶ In March he is taken on at Auguste Perret's (1874–1954) architectural firm in Paris, where he works for 14 months. During this time, he visits the museums of Paris, Rouen and Le Havre.

1910 ▶ Back in La Chaux-de-Fonds, Jeanneret works on a project for the Ateliers d'art réunis. Appointed by the Art School to study the decorative arts in Germany, from October 1910 to March 1911, he works as a draftsman at Peter Behrens' (1886–1940) studio in Neubabelsberg. He begins writing *La Construction des villes* and, in Munich, meets the writer William Ritter (1867–1955).

1911 ▶ In the company of art historian Auguste Klipstein (1885–1951), he embarks on a "journey to the East." His impressions are published in the newspaper *La Feuille d'avis de La Chaux-de-Fonds*.

1912 ▶ He runs the "new department" of the La Chaux-de-Fonds Art School and works on a freelance basis as an interior decorator and architect at no. 54, rue Numa-Droz. He produces sets of furniture and builds the Villa Jeanneret-Perret in La Chaux-de-Fonds and the Villa Favre-Jacot in Le Locle, Switzerland. He publishes his *Étude sur le mouvement d'art décoratif en Allemagne*.

1913 ▶ He exhibits a series of drawings entitled *Le Langage des pierres* (The Language of Stones) in Zurich.

1914 ▶ He travels in Alsace, Lorraine and the Rhineland, and visits the Werkbund exhibition in Cologne. With Max du Bois, Jeanneret becomes interested in reinforced-concrete constructions and devises the "Dom-ino" system. He works on the Les Crêtets Garden City, in La Chaux-de-Fonds, as well as on interiors.

1915 ▶ He stops working on *La Construction des villes* and *France-Allemagne*. He designs interiors for Hermann and Ernest-Albert Ditisheim.

1916 ► In La Chaux-de-Fonds, Jeanneret converts the Scala Cinema and builds the Villa Schwob.

1917 ► In Paris he founds the Société des applications du béton armé (SABA), and designs slaughterhouses in Challuy and Garchisy and a workers' housing development in Saint-Nicolas d'Aliermont, all of which are in France. He constructs a water tower in Podensac, Gironde, in southwestern France. He moves to no. 20, rue Jacob, and opens his first studio, at no. 13, rue de Belzunce.

1918 ► With the painter Amédée Ozenfant (1886–1966), Jeanneret writes the manifesto *Après le cubisme*. He paints *La Cheminée*, his first painting. He and Ozenfant exhibit at the Thomas Gallery, Paris, in December.

1919 ► Jeanneret designs the "Monol" house and draws up plans for workers' housing complexes (never realized).

1920 ► Together with the poet Paul Dermée (1888–1951), Ozenfant and Jeanneret found the review *L'Esprit nouveau*. Jeanneret elects to sign an article with the pseudonym "Le Corbusier," and designs the "Citrohan" house.

1921 ► He travels to Rome with Ozenfant.

1922 ► At the Salon d'Automne, Le Corbusier exhibits the "Ville contemporaine pour trois millions d'habitants" and his plans for the *immeuble-villas* project. He also builds the Villa Besnus in Vaucresson, France. He opens an office at no. 29, rue d'Astorg, with his cousin Pierre Jeanneret (1896–1967). They work together until 1940.

1923 ► He publishes *Vers une architecture*. He designs a house for his parents, the Villa "Le Lac" in Corseaux on Lake Geneva, completed in 1925, and in Paris builds Ozenfant's studio and the Villa La Roche-Jeanneret.

1924 ► Opens an office at no. 35, rue de Sèvres, in Saint-Germain-des-Prés, Paris. The Lipchitz-Miestschaninoff and Ternisien Houses are built in Boulogne-sur-Seine. He constructs workers' housing in Pessac for the Bordeaux-based industrialist Henri Frugès (1879–1974).

1925 ► At the Paris Exposition internationale des arts décoratifs, in the "L'Esprit nouveau" Pavilion, he presents dioramas of the "Contemporary City" and the Plan Voisin. He publishes *Urbanisme, L'Art décoratif d'aujourd'hui* and, with Ozenfant, *La Peinture moderne*.

1926 ► Georges-Edouard Jeanneret-Gris dies on April 11. Le Corbusier builds the Cook House in Boulogne-sur-Seine and the Church House in Ville d'Avray. He commences work on the design of the Villa Stein-de Monzie in Garches, completed in 1928. He publishes the *Almanach d'architecture moderne*. The Deutscher Werkbund commissions two houses from him for its Weissenhofsiedlung in Stuttgart. For the occasion he postulates his *Five Points for a New Architecture* (1927).

1927 ► His project for the competition to build the headquarters of the League of Nations in Geneva is rejected, prompting him to publish *Une Maison, un palais* in 1928.

1928 ► Le Corbusier receives the commission for the Centrosoyus Building in Moscow, which takes until 1936 to complete. The founding of the Congrès internationaux d'architecture moderne (CIAM) in La Sarraz, Vaud canton, Switzerland, provides a new platform for him.

1929 ► He travels to South America; his lectures held there are published in *Précisions* in 1930. He designs low-cost steel housing and, at the Salon d'Automne, he exhibits furniture designed with Charlotte Perriand and Pierre Jeanneret.

1930 ► Le Corbusier becomes a French citizen on September 19. On December 18, in Paris, he marries Yvonne Gallis (1892–1957). He designs a plan of Moscow, resumed under the title *La Ville radieuse*. In Paris he works on the Swiss Pavilion for the Cité universitaire and on the Cité de refuge for the Salvation Army. Willy Boesiger and Oscar Storonov publish the first of their eight-volume *Œuvre complète*.

1931 ► He finishes the Villa Savoye in Poissy. For Hélène de Mandrot, CIAM patroness, he builds a house in Le Pradet, near Toulon. In March he gives lectures in Algiers, and discovers the cities of the M'zab. He founds the journal *Plans*.

1932 ► He presents the Plan Obus for Algiers. His proposal for the Palace of the Soviets in Moscow is rejected. For the Genevan industrialist Edmond Wanner he constructs the Clarté Building, with an all-steel structure.

1933 ► His proposals for apartment buildings in Zurich for the Swiss Rentenanstalt and the terraced housing project on the Oued Ouchaïa in Algiers remain unrealized, as do the plans for Antwerp, Geneva and Stockholm. In Athens, Le Corbusier takes part in the fourth CIAM, whose theme is the "Functional City."

1934 ▸ Le Corbusier constructs an apartment building on rue Nungesser-et-Coli, in Paris, into which he incorporates his own studio apartment. He visits the FIAT plants in Turin and the new towns in the Pontine marshes and contributes to the monthly *Prélude*.

1935 ▸ He builds a house for Albin Peyron in Les Mathes and the "little weekend house" (Petite Maison) in La Celle-Saint-Cloud. He publishes *La Ville radieuse* and *Aircraft*. He proposes a city-planning project for the Zlín Valley, in Moravia, Czechoslovakia. His first trip to the United States, an account of which appears in *Quand les cathédrals étaient blanches*, published in 1937, is a disappointment.

1936 ▸ Back in Rio, he works with Lucio Costa and a group of young Brazilians on the Ministry of Health and Education, which is completed in 1944. He devises a plan for the reconstruction of Block no. 6 in Paris, which has become unfit for habitation, and a "stadium for popular demonstrations" for a suburb of the French capital.

1937 ▸ He is made a knight of the Légion d'honneur. After working on a housing project at the Kellermann Bastion and a "Center of Contemporary Aesthetics" at the Porte Maillot in Paris, Le Corbusier constructs, for the 1937 Paris Exposition internationale the "Les Temps nouveaux" Pavilion. He organizes the fifth CIAM, whose theme is "Housing and Leisure."

1938 ▸ He works on a skyscraper for the dock area of Algiers. He publishes *Des Canons, des munitions? Merci! Des logis, svp*. His projects for a "Great Square" and for the renovation of the Saint-Cloud bridge in Boulogne-sur-Seine are not realized.

1940 ▸ Dautry, French Minister of Armaments, commissions him to build a munitions factory in Aubusson. The office is closed down in June; Le Corbusier and Pierre Jeanneret part ways. Le Corbusier takes refuge in Ozon, where he works on plans for a factory and its housing units in Lannemezan and a system of school buildings that could be dismantled with Jean Prouvé. He becomes interested in sculpture.

1941 ▸ Le Corbusier goes to live in Vichy in January, where he finds some of his friends associated with Marshal Pétain's government. In May, he is entrusted with a temporary comission for the Committee for the Study of Housing and Construction. He publishes *Sur les quatre routes* and *Destin de Paris*.

1942 ▸ In July, Le Corbusier leaves Vichy. He publishes *Les Constructions Murondin* and *La Maison des hommes*.

1943 ▸ Le Corbusier publishes *La Charte d'Athènes* and *Entretien avec les étudiants des écoles d'architecture*.

1944 ▸ After the liberation, Le Corbusier chairs the City-Planning Committee of the Architects' National Front, stemming from the Resistance. The rue de Sèvres office is reopened in August.

1945 ▸ He designs the reconstruction plan for the city of Saint-Dié, and those for the cities of Saint-Gaudens and La Rochelle-La Pallice, none of which is realized. He publishes *Les trois établissements humains* and takes a second trip to the United States.

1946 ▸ Begins to make designs for the Marseilles Unité d'habitation. With the Breton cabinetmaker Joseph Savina he produces his first sculptures. He pub-

lishes *Manière de penser l'urbanisme* and *Propos d'urbanisme*.

1947 ▸ The United Nations appoints him as expert to the Building Committee for its Headquarters in New York City. The plans drawn up by Wallace Harrison borrow from several of Le Corbusier's ideas.

1948 ▸ For Edouard Trouin, he designs an underground basilica in La Sainte-Baume and starts the Currutchet House project in La Plata, Argentina. He designs his first tapestry cartoons.

1949 ▸ He works on the Bogota development plan. He designs the Roq and Rob holiday resorts in Roquebrune-Cap Martin.

1950 ▸ Le Corbusier publishes the first volume of his book on the "Modulor." The Indian government entrusts him with planning the city of Chandigarh. He publishes *Poésie sur Alger*.

1951 ▸ He draws up the master plan for Chandigarh and the public buildings forming its Capitol. He presents the "Modulor" system at a seminar held at the Milan Triennale, whose theme is "Divine Proportion."

1952 ▸ The Marseilles Unité d'habitation is inaugurated on October 14. For his own use Le Corbusier builds a small house at Roquebrune-Cap Martin. He completes the Duval factory in Saint-Dié. He draws up plans for the Governor's Palace in Chandigarh, which are ultimately abandoned.

1954 ▸ He designs the building of the Millowners' Association in Ahmedabad, India. He starts work on the Maison du Brésil at the Cité universitaire, Paris,

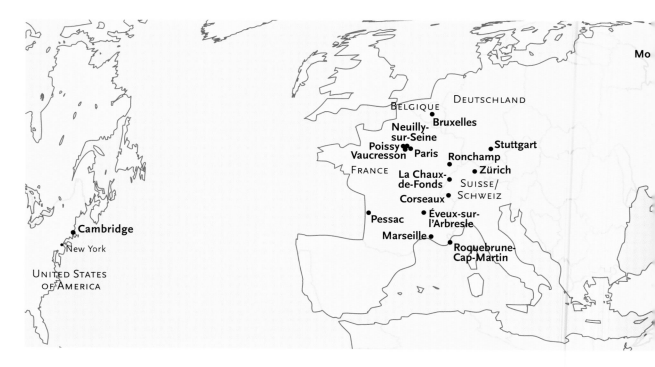

based on designs by Lucio Costa. He publishes *Une Petite Maison*.

1955 ► Le Corbusier finishes the Jaoul Houses in Neuilly-sur-Seine and the church in Ronchamp. In Chandigarh the High Court is inaugurated by Jawaharlal Nehru. The Nantes-Rezé Unité d'habitation is finished in June. The Sarabhai House is completed in Ahmedabad. He publishes *Le Poème de l'angle droit* and *Le Modulor 2 (La parole est aux usagers)*.

1956 ► In Ahmedabad he completes the Shodhan House. *Les Plans de Paris 1922–1956* is published.

1957 ► He designs the National Museum of Western Art in Tokyo, completed in 1959. His wife, Yvonne, dies on October 5 in Paris.

1958 ► He finishes the Secretariate in Chandigarh. At the Exposition universelle in Brussels, he erects the Philips Pavilion.

He builds the Berlin-Charlottenburg Unité d'habitation and takes part in the competition for the city's center.

1959 ► Harvard University commissions him to design the Carpenter Center for the Visual Arts, completed in 1962.

1960 ► Marie-Charlotte-Amélie Jeanneret, née Perret, dies on February 15. The Dominican Monastery of La Tourette, the designs for which Le Corbusier had begun in 1953, is consecrated in October. He publishes *L'Atelier de la recherche patiente*.

1961 ► He builds the Briey-en-Forêt Unité d'habitation. He designs a hotel and conference center on the site of the Orsay railway station in Paris.

1962 ► The Musée d'art moderne in Paris holds a retrospective of Le Corbusier's lifework. Heidi Weber commissions the architect to build an

exhibition pavilion in Zurich, which is completed in 1967.

1964 ► He designs a computer center for Olivetti in Rhô, Italy, the Strasbourg Conference Center and the French Embassy in Brasília. André Malraux, then Minister of Culture, commissions him to build a "Museum of the 20th Century" in Nanterre. Le Corbusier creates new designs for a hospital in Venice.

1965 ► He completes the Firminy Cultural Center, while the adjacent Unité d'habitation is finished in 1967 and the stadium in 1968. Work on the Church of Saint-Pierre, designed with José Oubrerie, comes to a halt and is not resumed until 2003. Le Corbusier dies on August 27 at Roquebrune-Cap Martin. André Malraux honors the architect with a funeral service in the Cour Carrée of the Louvre on September 1.

ROSSIA

NIHON
● Tōkyō

● Chandīgarh

BHARAT
● Ahmadābād

Map of the World

Belgium
Brussels
▸ Philips Pavilion (destroyed)

France
Eveux-sur-l'Arbresle
▸ Sainte-Marie-de-la-Tourette
Marseilles
▸ Unité d'habitation
Neuilly-sur-Seine
▸ Jaoul Houses
Paris
▸ Villa La Roche-Jeanneret
▸ "L'Esprit nouveau" Pavilion (destroyed)
▸ Cité de refuge
▸ Residential Building at Porte Molitor
Pessac
▸ Modern Frugès Quarter
Poissy
▸ Villa Savoye
Ronchamp
▸ Church of Notre-Dame-du-Haut
Roquebrune-Cap Martin
▸ "Le Cabanon"
Vaucresson
▸ Villa Stein-de Monzie

Germany
Stuttgart
▸ Weissenhofsiedlung

India
Ahmedabad
▸ Shodhan House
Chandigarh
▸ High Court
▸ Secretariate
▸ Assembly

Japan
Tokyo
▸ National Museum of Western Art

Russia
Moscow
▸ Centrosoyus Building

Switzerland
Corseaux (Vevey)
▸ Villa "Le Lac"
La Chaux-de-Fonds
▸ Fallet House
▸ Villa Jeanneret-Perret
▸ Villa Schwob
Zurich
▸ Le Corbusier Center

United States
Cambridge, Massachusetts
▸ Carpenter Center for the Visual Arts

Bibliography

Books by Le Corbusier
▶ Vers une architecture. G. Crès & Cie, Paris, 1923. English ed.: Towards a New Architecture. John Rodker, London, 1927.
▶ L'Art décoratif d'aujourd'hui. G. Crès & Cie, Paris, 1925. English ed.: The Decorative Art of Today. Architectural Press, London, 1987.
▶ Urbanisme. G. Crès & Cie, Paris, 1925. English ed.: The City of Tomorrow and Its Planning. John Rodker, London, 1929.
▶ Précisions sur un état présent de l'architecture et de l'urbanisme. G. Crès & Cie, Paris, 1930. English ed.: Precisions on the Present State of Architecture and City Planning. MIT Press, Cambridge, MA, 1991.
▶ La Ville radieuse. Editions de l'Architecture d'aujourd'hui, Boulogne, 1935. English ed.: The Radiant City: Elements of a Doctrine of Urbanism to be Used as the Basis of Our Machine-Age Civilization. Orion Press, New York, 1967.
▶ Quand les cathédrales étaient blanches. Plon, Paris, 1937. English ed.: When the Cathedrals were White: A Journey to the Country of Timid People. Routledge, London, 1947.
▶ Sur les quatre routes. Gallimard, Paris, 1941. English ed.: The Four Routes. Dobson, London, 1947.
▶ Les trois établissements humains. Denoël, Paris, 1945.
▶ Le Modulor. Editions de l'Architecture d'aujourd'hui, Boulogne, 1950. English ed.: The Modulor: A Harmonious Measure to the Human Scale, Universally Applicable to Architecture and Mechanics. Faber and Faber, London, 1951.
▶ Le voyage d'Orient. Editions Forces vives, Paris, 1966. English ed.: Journey to the East. MIT Press, Cambridge, MA, 1987.

General Books about Le Corbusier
▶ Boesiger, Willy (ed.): The complete works of Le Corbusier, 8 vols., Girsberger/Artemis, Zurich, 1930–1975.
▶ Petit, Jean: Le Corbusier lui-même. Editions Rousseau, Geneva, 1970.
▶ von Moos, Stanislaus: Le Corbusier, Elements of a Synthesis. MIT Press, Cambridge, MA, 1979.
▶ Brooks, H. Allen (ed.): The Le Corbusier Archive, 32 vols. Garland, New York/Fondation Le Corbusier, Paris, 1984.

▶ Lucan, Jacques (ed.): Le Corbusier: une encyclopédie. Centre Georges Pompidou, Paris, 1987.
▶ Benton, Tim (ed.): Le Corbusier: Architect of the Century. Arts Council of Great Britain, Londres, 1987.
▶ Gans, Deborah: The Le Corbusier Guide. Princeton Architectural Press, New York, 1987.
▶ William Curtis. Le Corbusier: Ideas and Forms. Phaidon, London, 1995.
▶ Baker, Geoffrey H. : Le Corbusier, the Creative Search, the Formative Years of Charles-Edouard Jeanneret. Van Nostrand Reinhold, New York, 1996.
▶ Frampton, Kenneth: Le Corbusier. Hazan, Paris, 2001.
▶ von Moos, Stanislaus et Arthur Rüegg (eds.): Le Corbusier before Le Corbusier: Applied Arts, Architecture, Painting, Photography. Yale University Press, New Haven, 2002.

Photo Credits